HERE IS

WHERE

I WALK

HERE IS

WHERE

I WALK

LESLIE CAROL ROBERTS

UNIVERSITY OF NEVADA PRESS *Reno & Las Vegas*

University of Nevada Press | Reno, Nevada 89557 USA

www.unpress.nevada.edu

Copyright © 2019 by University of Nevada Press

All rights reserved

Cover art by Yuval Helfman | Dreamstime.com

Cover design by Matt Strelecki

All photos are by the author unless otherwise indicated.

LIBRARY OF CONGRESS CATALOGING-IN-PUBLICATION DATA

Names: Roberts, Leslie Carol, author.

Title: Here is where I walk : episodes from a life in the forest / Leslie Carol Roberts.

Description: Reno ; Las Vegas : University of Nevada Press, [2019] |

Identifiers: LCCN 2018051396 (print) | LCCN 2018052307 (ebook) | ISBN 9781948908085 (ebook) | ISBN 9781948908078 (pbk. : alk. paper)

Subjects: LCSH: Roberts, Leslie Carol–Travel–California–Presidio of San Francisco. | Presidio of San Francisco (Calif.)–History. | Presidio of San Francisco (Calif.)–Description and travel.

Classification: LCC F869.S38 (ebook) | LCC F869.S38 P7474 2019 (print) | DDC 979.4/61–dc23

LC record available at https://lccn.loc.gov/2018051396

The paper used in this book meets the requirements of American National Standard for Information Sciences — Permanence of Paper for Printed Library Materials, ANSI/ NISO Z39.48-1992 (R2002).

FIRST PRINTING

Manufactured in the United States of America

FOR MY CHILDREN, WILL AND TYLER.

TABLE OF CONTENTS

INTRODUCTION

Nature is what we see—the hill, the afternoon, squirrel, eclipse, the bumblebee. Nay, nature is heaven. Nature is what we hear . . .
—Emily Dickinson

T here are reports in the esteemed journal *Nature* that scientists have discovered what is called the Wood Wide Web, a revelation that trees and fungi converse, sharing across species information about their needs and alerting each other to predation threats. Living in the midst of one of America's great historic forests—a forest with the same designation as historic human-built structures, these discoveries confirmed what I believe so many of us walkers-of-woods have long sensed. For what is a walk in a forest if not a chance to fully and deeply celebrate the sauntering and reflective mind? The brain hopping like some nimble coyote over rocks bridging a river? Legs astride. Arms lifting a drink of cool water to lips, water dripping down chin. Minty floral scent of the eucalyptus tree, indifferent and slightly smug robins hopping on the trailside.

"Joseph Baermann Strauss, the chief structural engineer for the Golden Gate Bridge, was also a poet."

The woods hold in abeyance the battering ram of time and the pressures and exigencies of modern life, they summon with reckless vigor memories of people alive and dead, loved and despised. The woods are not a quiet place, we walkers of the forest know, and it is this cacophony we seek in this nature we love. We should all be at the barricades lobbying for these places of solace and interiority, these places complex and cruel, these places that need and don't need us that can be obliterated by grasping gangrenous developers, these places that will yet exist as memory and whose pieces as seed and spore will return or relocate or represent in new ways. And so the forest is a place of blind, muscular hope.

The Presidio of San Francisco is a heavily forested and densely historical urban national park, and each walk and vista offers a performance of place almost noisy with varied voices—both of the woods and not. There is the backdrop of Army architecture and some moments where design aesthetics were privileged over military bureaucracy, and these buildings have a particular resonance. First human activities date back 10,000 years, and archeologists have unearthed evidence that the Ohlone people lived here as early as 740 AD. Fringe marshlands were home to small villages of seasonal and more permanent settlements, which ended when the Spanish military, civilians, and a single Franciscan priest arrived in 1776 to set up a presidio, or garrison.

They arrived by land, 193 civilians, 1,000 head of cattle, traveling from Sonora, Mexico. There were presidios erected across what is now called California, and the San Francisco Bay encampment faced particular challenges in the lack of arable land, the inhospitable winds and sand, and the fast habitat destruction brought on by cattle grazing.

The Presidio was controlled from 1776 until 1822 by the Spanish and then by Mexico until the United States took over in 1846. In 1972, the Golden Gate National Recreation Area was created, and includes the Presidio, Alcatraz, and Muir Woods in its 76,500 acres, making it one of the largest urban national parks in the world. There are 800 acres of open space in the Presidio, or 54 percent of its total, and 145 acres support remnant native plant communities ranging from wildflowers to oak woodlands. Sixteen rare plant species make their home here, including five protected by the Endangered Species Act. In 1996 Congress created the Presidio Trust, transferring eighty percent of the former military post to its jurisdiction (the National Park Service manages the shoreline perimeters.) A board was set up, appointed by the president of the United States, and the Presidio charter was written dictating that the Presidio had to preserve what was in its jurisdiction and also figure out how to build and maintain non-federal financial support. If they failed to do so, the Presidio could be sold off as excess land. This meant that the buildings and sites needed to be repurposed to bring in tenants—nonprofits and for-profits, residents and tourists. This was an experiment of sorts—the first park with an economic mission to support itself without government aid. (The Presidio hit this goal in 2013, by the way.)

The Presidio forest is mature trees and these days a wave of younger trees—part of a forest-replenishment plan—eucalyptus, pines, cypress, planted from the 1880s through the 1940s by the US Army and slowly aging out. During the 218 years the Presidio was an Army post, tree planting was a way to shield both from the wind and weather and a way to create theater—the grand and mysterious might of a militarized Presidio masked from civilian view by dense woods. The forest today is surrounded by major roadways, including Highway 101, which tunnel through and bisect and frame it on two sides. Several of the famed stands of trees have been entirely removed and replanted because crowding had left the mature trees unhealthy and weak, prone to falling during winter wind storms. You can easily spy the sick trees on a walk in these woods: They have very long, scrawny trunks and a thin, wide canopy—a desperate reach in a dense wood towards light needed to survive. They have the same affect as starving humans, elongated and sinewy, forms folding in peculiar ways.

There is a resonance and sense of awe in these woods, the forest's determined survival against the odds: how the trees define the 1,480 acres of park, trees laced with hiking trails, ringed by sandy beaches and soaring cliffs and vistas, trees tucked into the northern corner of San Francisco, patrolled by coyotes, skunks, and raptors, banana slugs slouching amidst scraps of euc leaves. Even as humans redesign the place to make it suited to modern recreation and corporate life and the arts—people in tight cycling kits roar around on road bikes, heaving plates of artisan tacos served with agave liquors, a museum celebrating the cartoons of Walt Disney; a corporate headquarters for the *Star Wars* artists complete with Yoda statue; the majestic forest dominates it all.

My family and I moved to the Presidio in 2005. We were coming home to San Francisco and our former neighborhood in the Mission had lost its charm for me. My mother-lens saw in high-relief how trash accumulated on sidewalks and around curbs, how on weekends crosswalks jammed with drunks in search of bacon-leavened donuts, mussels and fries or whatever the latest food craze might be—was no place for me to rear young children.

From the first days in the Presidio, I walked the woods. In the beginning, the Presidio was underpopulated and the homes were in ill repair. The only other walkers were a diplomat from the local South Korean consulate—always nattily attired in a shiny silver suit and bright tie—and a Buddhist monk in an orange robe. We would smile and nod at each other.

On these many years of walks, over the months, the forest has given me ample time to commune with the place and with my own memories. I don't doubt that the trees are in conversation with each other; and I don't doubt that they are also speaking to me. Trees are wonderful companions in thinking, and they provide a particular aesthetic that has caused artists, writers, and naturalists across the years to pause and ponder how glorious a tree is in all its singular characteristics.

There is a particular cypress tree I look at each day, morning and night. It stands at the top of the dunes immediately behind my house. It is a tangled messy tree, using a strategy leveraging half cracked off, huge lower branches to serve as support against the rough Pacific winter storms. This quality often prompts guests to ask if I should hire an arborist to trim these unsightly branches, to facilitate my view west, an otherwise open shot across the Pacific Ocean to the Farallon Islands. I then explain what the tree is up to, how it accommodates the weather and wind with its plan to press fallen limbs in a sort of skirt around its base. I also explain that without the tree, the wind and rain would blast me and the already quivering window panes might be inclined to blow right out here on top of the dunes.

So the tree, I conclude, has my back, and my story of its needs is a way for me to have its back in turn.

Seeing beauty in a fallen limb, observing an Anna's hummingbird alight on a tendril; tracing the path of the great-horned owl as it finds its place as night falls: All of this artistry is given to me by this one cypress tree. And I am grateful for it.

I also found the trees eased my mind. I would turn away from the mundane anxieties of life as a single mother in an expensive city, and in turn flow towards ideas about art, about my own life as a creative, from girlhood walks and studio art classes, to reporting the news in far-flung places like Antarctica, to the elations of my children's births and young lives, to the sadness of people lost along the path. So the forest came to be a place for me to hear my own story and when I returned from my walks, sometimes with fresh jottings in a small brown notebook, I would sit down for an hour or so, in the bright morning light, and put down these thoughts. Or I would wait for my children to fall asleep and then I would sit at my Steelcase desk, a greenish-grey desk, pushed against the window and in the dark stare at my tree and bash out words as they came to mind. And so. I embrace this conversation fomented and encouraged by the trees and for the fact that each walk in each forest or wood is an interaction singular and rich.

EPISODE ONE

In all things of nature, there is something of the marvelous.
—Aristotle

The caribou feeds the wolf, but it is the wolf who keeps the caribou strong. —Keewatin Inuit saying

January: On Coyotes

The sun rises on us all in the Presidio National Park, the coyotes, the doves, the hummingbirds, the raptors, the slugs, the humans, the waves crashing on Baker Beach, and it is in this light I walk. The early morning finds the last of the nocturnal species still picking around, and so it is the coyote who is my companion as the edge of the continent clicks into another day. Grey and rusty coats, curious and hesitant, focused and yet opportunistic, the coyote: I can relate.

Coyotes are a spotlight species because of their dazzling adaptations to shifting climate, urban footprints, food sources, on a seemingly ineluctable march across the planet. They have patrolled the land called North America for at least 10,000 years. In the twentieth century, the coyote moved from prairies, deserts, and grasslands to forests fanning out across North America. By the 1990s, the coyote arrived on the East Coast and now lives in New York City. The coyote is a species benefiting from the retreat of apex predators (although don't we all?), which is true with an asterisk: The coyote has made it to Alaska where there are plenty of wolves and yet the coyote gets purchase. The coyote is headed south, towards the South American continent. All this raises a core philosophical question: Do we imagine this expanded range for the coyote to be a natural evolution, based on skill and adaptation? Or do we imagine this expansion to be unnatural? In the end, the fact of coyote in Central Park or the Presidio forest may be our answer.

For all their adaptive prowess, coyotes possess two known weaknesses. They are heavy sleepers, making them easy to creep up on, and they tend to look back over their shoulders when running for their lives. This looking back slows them down, making them vulnerable to being shot or otherwise caught. Given their renowned land speed—a robust 65 kilometers an hour at top speed—this looking-back habit strikes as worthy of consideration. They must be aware of their fleet-footed advantage. Has this evolved a certain arrogance, or sense, it is OK to slow down because no one and nothing is going to catch up?

No one knows for sure how coyotes came back to the Presidio, but they do believe it was sometime in 2002. I know how I got here: I had to move back to San Francisco from Iowa City, where I was teaching and living in a house with a white-picket fence because it was important for my children to live close to father, too. I did not dispute this notion that proximate parents are good for children, I just wanted to stay in Iowa. I loved the pale greenish-blue hydrangeas in spring and how at local cafés people asked quite genuinely how each other's writing or painting or filmmaking was going. In Iowa, people have time to ask that question and to hear the answer; it is not a commercial question, and no one cares if you are not done with your work; no one says, *where might I have seen your work?* I loved how I could afford to live there and how there was no traffic and I could write every day and not stop and panic that I might die broke and alone, a horrible burden on my children, because I was squandering so much of my professor's salary on things like food and shelter. It's the making of the work that is interesting, and that is why we ask and listen to the answer.

I read speculation that the first coyotes trotted over the Golden Gate Bridge at night from Marin County. Picture that: a couple of them loping along that orange oxide bridge. Who told them the Army had retreated, and all of the buildings were largely devoid of soldiers and there were abundant moles to feast on?

The Presidio is mindful of all residents and their health and safety—preserving species is part of its charter—and there were soon signs advising all who passed to drive with care. Coyote crossing. Not long after, I began to see coyotes crossing the road by one of the signs near my house. I guess coyotes can read, too.

My son, Will, was completing grammar school and my daughter, Helena, was in third grade and they attended different schools, so after walking with the coyotes my morning was about shuttling to schools and engaging with drop-off systems. The schools designed drop-off systems to create maximum car flow—parents in orange vests would wave cars to the curb, like we were 737s taking off from O'Hare. The car door would be pulled open, and the children would pop out, all heavy backpacks and lunch totes and rolled-up artwork. It was so much more complicated than life in Iowa or New Zealand. In the afternoons, the same drill in reverse, so I calculated I had about four and a half hours of writing time and chore time before I had to get back in the car and do this in reverse. I never calculated how many hours of my life were spent driving around San Francisco, dropping off or picking up children at school or sports or plays. But I do know when people ask me why I have not finished more books or written ten screenplays and an HBO show, a part of me wants to scream, I never mastered driving and writing at the same time.

There were days when I arrived early for pick-up and would park my car and then I would wait with the others—many of the designated drivers were nannies, I quickly learned—and then I would hear other sorts of things that would distract me. One in particular struck me: At my son's school, a mother was lamenting the fact that because of a measly snowfall at Lake Tahoe, they were not going to be able to use the enormous house they had built so the kids could enjoy ski week in the Sierras. All three of her children wanted to be on the ski team, then no snow! Instead, they all had to fly to Austria to ski. This statement fixated in my mind, and I told and retold her lament to friends in Iowa and New Zealand when they emailed and called me. It was a Margaret Mead moment. *I shall always be an outsider,* I would moan. I walked in the cool woods and watched the turbulent ocean pound the dark sand and thought about how to unpack the ski-mother's lament. Was it funnier that it was a complaint or that the teller was clueless as to how it came off to the average listener? Was it funnier when you find out she was also carrying a $2,000 handbag to pick up her sons at school? Was it funnier that when she asked me what I was doing for ski week, I said I was counting coyotes in the Presidio because I am writing a report on them and I found out that their piss smells really, really strong, which is how they marked their territory, and she laughed and told me how funny I am.

Coyotes, *canis latrans,* eat mice, rats, gophers, insects, reptiles, carrion, amphibians, wild fruit with blueberries being a particular favorite, birds and their eggs, and pets; they hunt solo, with a companion, or in small packs. Its name is a Spanish adaptation of an Aztec word, *coyotl.* They are found in abundance across California, however they do well across North America, and have extended their reach from the near-Arctic to Panama. Sometimes they play with their prey before they kill and eat it. Coyotes are relatives to the wolf, fox, dog, and jackal. Long jumpers—up to four meters—coyotes adapt well to a changing environment—they are a species seemingly designed for change.

I liked how adaptable they were: If need be, they dig their own burrows, or co-opt other animals' burrows, digging and shaping it to fit their needs. I also noted how they had more than a few similarities to humans, how they adjusted their hunting style to their prey, for instance. Their rough, wild-animal qualities included producing strong-smelling urine to mark their territory, and yellow, black-irised eyes that one writer noted, gives them a cunning look.

Most of us will call to mind the coyote's best-known trait, its yelping howl, a series of high-pitched squeals. It was peculiar to learn no one knows exactly why the coyote cries out so dramatically. Some believe it may be purely social. First one

coyote calls out, then another replies? Then many voices join in? It's a mystery akin to the people standing outside a grammar school in San Francisco plotting expensive trips to European ski resorts because children have decided they want to be on a ski team.

Coyote hunting moles in my neighborhood during pupping season.

While I hold them dear, coyotes are not universally beloved. They might even be called controversial because they have a habit of killing and eating small farm animals and attacking pets if they feel threatened.

In my experience, coyotes are inclined towards loping along with an aura that suggests they are shy. There were two in my backyard, and they got spooked by an Anna's hummingbird and ran off as if the tiny bird was going to take them down. Not long after the cowardly coyote incident, I was driving home from the grocery store and found a coyote standing in the middle of Arguello Boulevard, across the street from the Presidio golf course, at the curve right before you hit the part of the road where there are no street lights because even urban forests are meant to be dark at night.

I stopped my car. It was late, and we were the only two on the dark road. She stared at me, captured in the bright lights, one paw raised. In the morning, this road would be busy with commuters funneling to and from the Golden Gate Bridge. But in the still blackness, in this instant, the tangled woods and empty macadam were ours alone. In the distance, the cry of the great horned owl on its nighttime patrol.

Not long afterwards, dog walkers reported a coyote lurking around the Presidio cemetery, jogging up behind them, lunging at pets. An agitated coyote then made a couple of appearances in a Presidio backyard, scaring a father and his young child, coming back later to have a go at their dog. After some discussion, a sharpshooter arrived, dispatched at the Presidio Trust's request. They killed the coyote. I called a friend at the Presidio Trust, who told me the coyote was the mother of pups holed up in a den close to the home and dog walker incidents. *All she was doing was protecting her pups,* she added. *Like any good mother would do. Get this; now the pups may starve to death. No one has seen the father.*

But coyotes practice monogamy and are loyal to one another. The pair makes a den, carefully tends the inside prior to the birth of pups, and cleans out waste after the pups' birth. The father patrols for food while the mother nurses then weans her pups. The father coyote cared for the pups alone. The pups survived.

The story of the single-father coyote trying to keep his pups alive occupied my mind and I sat on a tree stump north of our home, contemplating the unexpected turn of events. The stump is quite large, it could fit two lawn chairs and serve as an organic deck. Fog slipped in around the trees. Eucalyptus leaves shivered.

The coyote's face staring at me in the darkness stuck in my mind; it did not have a cunning expression. It seemed rather disengaged with me—more interested in getting on its way.

As I contemplated this gaze, I recalled spending an evening a few years back in Utah in a session with a woman advertised as an empath or a clairvoyant and a spiritual guide. I was with my friend Linda, and we were escaping the day-to-day

work of being mothers of young children, hiking and spa-
ing in the red rock desert. The red rock desert is a marvelous
place to walk with a friend, and we walked and talked about
the novels we were reading. We both read a lot of novels.
We would hike twelve hilly, red miles each morning, the sun
already beginning to blaze by 9 a.m., and then sit by the hotel
pool under umbrellas in the afternoon or flounder around in
kick-boxing classes, trying to imitate the instructor's furious
roundhouse kicks while we studiously avoided having our
body fat calibrated by a man we dubbed Mr. Clean because he
was tall, muscular, and wore a tight, white outfit. Mr. Clean
had freaked me out on the first or second day when I agreed
to sit in his office and answer a few questions. He started
by studying my hands and feet, and then he made some
proclamations about me and asked me to answer true or false.
*You prefer your food at room temperature. True. You prefer not
to have ice in your drinks. True. You prefer vegetables to meat.
True. You choose salty foods over sweet foods. True. You first had
your period at age sixteen. True.* After this last proclamation,
I mumbled something about needing to use the bathroom
and sprinted off to find Linda, to warn her. After that, Mr.
Clean would fax us in our suite: *You have not yet had your
complimentary nutritional analysis. You need to take Vitamin
K. I can tell by your hand analysis,* which would make us
laugh nervously, making jokes about how he was outside in
the hall, waiting. The faxes always came in the evening, and
fax technology was obsolete. When they came clicking and
buzzing in, we were always seated on the floor, having a picnic
of sorts, a chardonnay Linda had uncorked, eating cheese
and olives, flipping through a stack of women's magazines,
discussing how photoshopped all the arms and abs were.

The spa offered "experiences"—climbing in Zion, trips to
Vegas dinner shows, an evening retreat with a spiritual guide
in a remote tent, a vague reference to a ritual that cleansed
participants' heads. I asked if the spiritual guide retreat was filled,
and the concierge, without looking at any list, said, *No it is not.*

This sinewy, pale concierge then pointed to a colorful brochure—yellow rafts catapulted by surging river waters, lengthy zip lines strung haphazardly from one remote red rock outcropping to another, and lines of bikes like so many beetles snaking through a narrow canyon. *This is what really defines the Utah experience,* he said, tapping a ballpoint pen on shiny photos of people in white helmets tied with ropes to a steep red rock wall. I squinted at the roped people's faces. They looked like leftover holiday decorations hanging forlornly in canyon shadows.

We smiled and declined and set off to walk our twelve miles, one foot in front of the other. No ropes needed.

Later that afternoon, lightly sunburned from the day's hike and a little pink-cheeked from some hasty chardonnay aperitifs in the suite, Linda and I joined a small group gathered in the hotel lobby. A battered white van pulled up and the six of us climbed in. The van was powdered with a light dusting of red rock dust and inside were three bench seats with missing seat belts. It was about thirty minutes to our destination, the driver said as we pulled out. The group chatted companionably. There was a classical flutist who had repetitive stress injury in one of her hands and came to the desert to heal it; a pair of sisters from New York City who worked as high school French teachers, had never been to Utah, and pointed out distant lights, making wisecracks about big houses and multi-wife families; and a young redhead with big earrings who had spent the afternoon by the hotel pool, talking on her cellphone and crying and begging her sister to call her married ex-boyfriend to find out why he broke it off.

Our spiritual guide, a woman with long, grey-streaked hair, exuded a certain cool indifference to the passengers' banter, sat in the front passenger seat with her visor flipped down, periodically glancing into the small mirror at the rest of us in the back. The driver was a heavily wrinkled man wearing a battered straw cowboy hat with a large hole in the brim. The hole was round and had blackened edges. It looked like a burn hole, like the hat had caught on fire. I was thinking about how this whole retreat seemed like bullshit. How it could never work with these strangers and that man with the hole in his hat. I hoped he was OK to drive and not drunk. Oh well, I thought, at least it would be entertaining. Maybe I could write about it. I turned my head and caught the eye of the spiritual guide in the visor mirror. She was staring at me intently, as if she could read my mind and raised one eyebrow at me. I recalled the brochure said she was an empath. She held my gaze for a moment then looked away. It looked like she had a smile on her face, a sort of disparaging smile.

For some reason, I felt ashamed of my thoughts. I wanted to be more positive. *There will be much to learn, much to see, so much to hear.* I repeated this silently as we bounced onto ever-rougher roads. The sun set and the air was cold and dry and there were no more lights on the horizon. The suspension in the van was shot so we started to hang onto the seat backs in front of us to keep from bouncing too high. The van had grown quiet.

The driver finally parked at a precipitous angle along the side of the road. *Walk down that path,* he said, pointing into the dark. And then the six of us were out of the van, scrambling down a narrow path to a lighted tent that seemed to appear from nowhere. *This is where they shoot us and bury us in a shallow grave,* Linda said in a hushed tone, as we picked our way along. Linda was a lawyer who had been on a Pac-12 crew team. I'd pick her on my side in a desert fight. *All we need to do is run faster than the French teachers and we'll get away,* I said.

Two smiling men welcomed us inside the lighted tent and handed us neatly folded fleece blankets, greeting each of us with gentle bows, something between a yoga bow and the acknowledgment of a minor member of a royal family. They then handed us each a ceramic, handleless mug of a hot herbal tea and instructed us to unfold the blanket on the ground, to sit in a circle on our blankets around a small pile of smoking herbs. The empath was walking around the tent, tending the smoking herbs, breathing deeply. She tied up her hair with a thin piece of leather and the two men arranged a small pile of blankets for her, so she could sit a bit off the ground. The assistants had long ponytails and each wore necklaces with their tight shirts, necklaces of leather and fangs and feathers. A perfect accessory, I reckoned, for a tent in the dark desert. *Anywhere else, completely ridiculous.* I pointed to my neck then pointed to their necks as I nudged Linda who was seated next to me. She gave me the thumbs up. One of the assistants asked us not to talk, then instructed us about the retreat. He explained how the spiritual guide needed us to clear our minds. I tried to silence the torrent of observations blasting across my brain like news updates on a Times Square marquee, the smoking herbs, which smelled like pot, the necklaces, the oiled ponytails. The fact that it was hot in the tent but neither of the assistants looked sweaty. Could feel a damp moustache of perspiration form on my upper lip.

You need to empty your minds of thoughts and allow her to guide you, one of them repeated, and then the two assistants sat very straight and closed their eyes. The leader had her eyes closed softly and appeared lost in thought. Were they empaths, too? I wondered. I closed my eyes and tried to think about nothing. *Nothing is hard to think about;* particularly because I kept recalling the look she gave me in the car.

When the guide began to speak, I peeked at her with one eye; she wore a peculiar, long, constructed piece around her neck. It was not exactly jewelry, it looked more . . .

Think of Nothing! I said to myself, breathing deeply and rhythmically. I tried to do as the assistants were doing, blowing out air through their mouths with a loud pfuff. I am thinking about Nothing. Not the thing around her neck *(What was it? Animal bones? Fur? Did it smell or itch? Where was it in the van?) Stop! Silence your brain.*

Then she talked to us for a while about spiritual traditions, a hodgepodge of ideas culled from the Indian subcontinent, Middle Eastern lore, poetry written in the 1960s in California. Part of what she said sounded like lyrics from a Grateful Dead song. She intoned how we could know more of the Earth; then she told us we must all stretch out our bodies to begin the journey. I lay back and folded my hands across my chest, not because we were told to do so but because that seemed like the proper, respectful way to behave. Then I wondered if thinking about how I was holding my arms was a little bit cynical. Then I tried not to laugh, which was hard, because I opened my eyes and looked at Linda and she was laughing next to me, soundlessly, mouth and eyes closed.

Breathe in, the guide told us in her lovely, theatrical voice. *Breathe in, and then I want you to imagine this: You are digging your way out of the Earth. Where will you come to the surface?*

In a meadow.

In a large meadow surrounded by trees.

Many animals live there.

Start digging. See who you meet.

I closed my eyes and imagined myself digging. I breathed in the fragrant, skunky smoke.

I was an efficient digger, it turned out, and soon had pulled myself from the tunnel through a hole and into the light—and I started walking across a gorgeous, green valley floor. It looked like something from a Mary Blair illustration—bright and flat and a little off kilter. I loved the place. I ran, tearing along, wind in my hair. For some reason, I wanted to explore the forest that lined the green valley. At the edge of the forest, I stopped and peered into the thick undergrowth, marveled at the dense tree canopy.

Then I saw the wolf watching me, body partially masked by the foliage, eyes locked on mine.

I stared back. We stood together in a valley. The wolf had dazzling blue eyes. She looked at me, and I looked at her. I felt relaxed and connected to the place, to the wolf, to the trees. Time stopped. All felt exactly as it should be. It was like I had come home to a place I never knew I had left.

It was startling when a human voice summoned me to come back, to open my eyes. I had no idea how much time had a passed—Hours?

Stretch your arms, she said. *Sit up when you are ready.*

As each of us gradually sat up and stretched, with sleepy faces and messy hair, we were told to report what we had seen and done on our expeditions.

The first woman, the classical flutist, explained in fairly fine detail how she had met three raccoons and a deer. The raccoons had been expecting her, the deer had not.

The pool-crier described purple and white birds with huge talons and beaks filled with branches of crimson flowers. One of her earrings had fallen off, and one of the assistants was helping her find it.

When it was my turn, I said, *well, I saw a green, green stretch of valley and there was a forest and there was a wolf with blue eyes.*

I talked a bit about the valley, how it looked geologically similar to Yosemite, the soaring granite edifices, the too-green trees. As I spoke the entire experience remained quite clear in my mind, as though I were describing a real place. I found myself going back to add details I forgot, like the white flowers with the yellow centers, which sounded like daisies but were closer in appearance to peonies. My listeners nodded. The details of the place were important.

But the spiritual guide was disinterested in the flowers and wanted me to repeat what I saw of the wolf: *What color were her eyes? What did she say? Did she seem engaged?*

I told her the wolf eyes were blue. Light, clear blue.

She said that this was an important connection for me because the wolf did not show herself often. She looked at her watch and she said we needed to move on to the next person. But she told me to keep one thing in mind: The wolf has something she wants those who see her to understand. Then the French teachers were asked what they saw. But I did not hear their answer, nor did I really listen to the banter in the van on the way back.

In our suite, with the pesky fax machine unplugged, we sat on the cool tile floor and had some wine. *That was definitely pot they were burning in that tent,* she said.

Do you think any of that stuff is true, I asked.

What part? You mean how the raccoons were talkative and the deer was not?

We laughed. That night, I lay awake on the cool sheets thinking about that wolf. How strange that it occupied my mind. It had all seemed so phony until it didn't.

When I got home to Iowa and my children, over a dinner of fish sticks and Tater Tots, I told them about the imaginary wolf encounter. We were sitting in the dining room I had painted orange oxide to match the Golden Gate Bridge, in our little Sears kit house, and my son, Will, who was eight at the time, sipped his milk and listened, intrigued by this.

So the next Saturday, he and I rode our bikes to the public library in downtown Iowa City, searched the children's section first, and then the adult sections, to find out about wolves. We learned that the Pawnee, who lived in what is now Nebraska, felt so aligned with the wolf that the hand signal for wolf was the same as the hand signal for Pawnee. Will pointed this out to me on an illustrated page, showing a wolf in a grasslands: They thought they were wolves. Maybe that's what the story meant, Mom.

We learned how Sirius, the wolf star, came and went in the night sky and how its disappearance and reappearance signified the star or the wolf's need for spiritual renewal. The language was unclear to me what was thought to be renewing. It reminded me of the night in the tent. We read on, how the Milky Way was the wolf's road and the wolf star loped along this road. My son grew bored with the wolf stories and wandered over to some computers where children gazed at glowing screens, arranging geometric shapes into stacks as they fell from the top of the screen.

At night in our Iowa backyard, in the small garden framed by a white picket fence, the sky was less occluded by the apricot glow of halogen lights—and the Milky Way beckoned to us. Oh, it dawned on me—because I am thick about interpretive exercises—perhaps I get it! *I am the wolf, and the wolf is me.* And this, surprisingly, did not feel false or like an over-reach. And in this spirit of happiness and understanding I went inside and urged my children to pause their movie and come out in their matching blue pajamas, to stand in the warm dark. I pointed out Sirius, the wolf of the night sky, and they lifted their heads and squinted for an instant before running back inside. I stood there alone in the dark on the slate patio, then I hurried through the side gate and into the dark and empty street to get a more wide-open view, away from the backyard trees, to see the wolf star unobscured by tangled black branches as it made its way across that peculiar mosaic of glistening, pale stars.

NOTEBOOK ONE

Natura nihil fit in frustra
Nature does nothing in vain.
"(O I see what I sought to escape, confronting, reversing my cries;
I see my own soul trampling down what it ask'd for.)"
—"Give Me the Splendid, Silent Sun," Walt Whitman

Here
Here Is
Here Is Where
Here Is Where I
Here Is Where I Walk

These words are my warm-up exercise before I start writing. I say them with reverb as though I am Fatboy Slim and then sometimes like I am Biggie Smalls, holding my mic at a jaunty angle; I say them in a monster voice. I improvise them as a way to get going with the voices in my head, the voices of my writing. Because it is a competition between walking and sitting down to write. Walking is not writing, although I can argue on any day that it is.

When I begin my research into the earliest days of colonial development of the Presidio, I wanted to see what it was they wanted to know, besides the front-line stories of colonialist instincts. Were they culture deserters, tired of Madrid, king, country, tired of the stench and poverty of Europe? Or did they seek some idea of forest and freedom? Or was I being completely naïve?

The diaries of Padre Pedro Font, a naturalist, artist, and Franciscan in northwest Mexico, offer a detailed view of the earliest days of the Presidio. Font was ordered by his superior to accompany Juan Bautista de Anza from San Miguel de Horcasitas, Mexico, to San Francisco, and back. He kept a detailed journal of this trip from September 1775, to June

1776. Font is described as a chunky man with a receding hairline, although why his hair matters in all this strikes me as peculiar. It has been noted that Font was ill for much of the journey, with sores in his mouth and a sense of irritation with the place, the peoples he met, and the people with whom he traveled. All this aside, he documents his view of that place, the beauty of wild flowers, his fear of grizzly bears.

"There are many of these beasts in that country, and they often attack and do damage to the Indians when they go to hunt, of which I saw many horrible examples," he wrote.

Later that year, in 1776, grizzlies aside, the Spanish set up San Francisco's Presidio. He climbs to the cliffs on the south side of the harbor, in what is now the Presidio National Park. "This place and its vicinity has abundant pasturage, plenty of firewood, and fine water, all good advantages for establishing here the presidio or fort which is planned. It lacks only timber, for there is not a tree on all those hills."

54 degrees F; wind from the south at 7 mph, cloudy. No surf of any note, waves press towards the beach with a force that says, lake. Huge coils of sea vegetables tangled, Medusa's hair, bulbs built as flotation devices, the color of oxidized bronze.

Fog obscures the red bridge, hills of Marin, pulls the horizon towards me. Sky moves in a gesture of embrace, come to me, it says, all you fog-bound beach walkers.

It is a still, wet January day, and I am hanging art in my Presidio home. The rain poured through the night, and the forest continues to shed water long after rain has abated so the tinny sound of water moving through the rain spout alongside the front door adds a loud, percussive note to the day—it's no longer raining, but the soundtrack suggests otherwise.

I am rehanging art on white walls. Periodically, I move pictures and drawings and photos around the home, so that when I write in bed, under the covers, from my bedside and at the foot of my bed, I have work to contemplate. What I am really compelled by these days is the act of drawing and painting the world. I used to do this, it used to be my main identity until I was about twenty. I recall why I stopped, and it is of no import. One fragment of conversation comes to mind, a painting teacher at Wayne State University, where I was an art major as a freshman, said to me: *You must be ready to divorce yourself from society to be an effective painter. You have to live within your art.*

This idea struck something deep inside me, and I recall wandering away from the studios on Wayne State's urban campus towards the old Motown Records building. Motown had long since fled for Los Angeles, but the name remained on the building. Many of the windows were broken and drapes or curtains floated through the shattered glass, frozen by ice into shapes or flapping in the wind. I was thinking about people serving other people and I was thinking about celebrity culture and I was thinking about how I did not want to spend my life alone with my paints and a canvas. What I did not have the ability to do was imagine that all creative work that means anything has this quality and that as I reimagined myself as a student of political science and a journalist who would report on power relationships and champion those on the lesser end, I would have a relationship with my work that was absolutely solitary. And that I would love this quality of writing, the time sitting on the floor, staring out the window, fingers flying over the black keys and then the words that would be printed out and I would have that experience where I see the plurality within myself, to remember that people are not monolithic and that we all encompass all.

As I turn over one of my large drawings, I see the carefully lettered entry card for the Hallmark Awards, entered when I was in high school, each line filled in with my neat hand, all capitals, with a black Pilot Razor Point pen. I won a gold key for this charcoal drawing of houseplants—a philodendron, a jade, a cutting of a philodendron in a six-sided glass jar. The drawing pulls my mind back to those days, I can still recall working on this piece of paper over many hours, with the still life arranged in a large, handled wooden box affixed with a small spotlight for better dark/light contrast.

The landscapes of my youth are lost—the first, the Maryland countryside, became an exurb of Washington, DC, with wider roads clogged with cars and lined with shopping malls and housing developments. The second, Detroit, is a better-documented story of human exodus from a geographically massive city and the slow, steady decline of the built environment. What's peculiar here is that we don't seem to have ever constructed exit strategies for built environments. We just build, like madmen on some mundane aesthetic kick and with no sense that we are ruining the world. I see people in a few hundred years, whatever is left of us, the nomadic tribes of people, sitting around and discussing what idiots we were, going all in on permanence. Like those sites unearthed from foliage, forgotten then rediscovered, where young virgins were sacrificed to make it rain.

When the first "art shots" of the decay of the once-grand buildings and blight were on display for people to view and remark on, I recall a strange, choking feeling in my throat. I stare intently at the pale celadon paper. I have never seen the same photographic interest in the destruction of the Maryland countryside. I see so clearly one butterfly packed meadow alongside Cashell Road.

How do we create a sensibility? These places unite in my sensibility, and I take the liberty of being an artist. I can be a kind of explorer, following my nose. It's a sense of openness, it's the idea that each person can have a broad sensibility. What I work to encourage in my students is that they have their moment of deciding what is a beautiful thing—you don't need to hate one kind of writing or design or art because you love another. Finding a reality for yourself is the point and in that understanding somewhere there is a truth—the thought that memories are real, that all work is a memoir, to understand that the imagined and the actual are always in conversation.

Landscape stories and landscape art and landscape design are always about distortion, interpretation, reverence. In varying proportions. If I believe, which I do, that the botanist Oliver Rackham had it right when he detailed four ways "landscape is lost"—through the loss of freedom, beauty, wildlife and vegetation, and meaning, I also believe that none of these losses triumphs over any of the others and that aesthetics, ecology, language, and human relational identity to a particular landscape each matter equally. The Presidio is a place where people come to seek refuge from The World, the immediate, larger city, and all of its technological and architectural innovation. *This is how we place ourselves into this landscape, and this is what we do when we get here.*

I listen to the wind hit the eucalyptus trees and watch ivy flutter along trunks. I also listen to talk radio, a scientist with a new book out is being interviewed. I am working to hear his comments as a collage.
We have this peculiar intimacy with all around us.
There is no such thing as nature.
We share DNA with onions.
What then comes to mind: A conversation with a geologist in New Zealand who said, *The main difference between you and a star is your water content.*

EPISODE TWO

Life does not consist mainly, or even largely, of facts and happenings. It consists mainly of the storm of thoughts that are forever blowing through one's mind. —Mark Twain

February: On Ecology Trail

A story of ecology: Ecology Trail winds down from Inspiration Point, a patio of neat stone, a piazza feel, an overlook I associate with the hills above Florence, Italy.

Serpentinite rock astride Ecology trail, a rudder of rock pushing up towards the sky.

Although the density of the trees will soon hide the trail and the sky from view it is easy from this vantage point to forget there are any trails at all and to imagine that the main purpose of Inspiration Point, indeed the entire hilltop, is to stand there and take in the famous, distracting view of the San Francisco Bay.

I often think about what a strange name ecology would be for a trail in the true wild and how it works so well for a trail in this designed forest called the Presidio. The Presidio is a place where anyone can learn about endangered or typical habitats. There is a sweet sincerity and intensity to the Presidio mission and a persistent invitation to join in and help with the restoration. Signs and apps and programs and videos, a deluge of opportunities. At Inspiration Point I pause with my thermos of coffee and sip from the small metal cap. It's indeed a phenomenon how the stories of some places catch on and the stories of others do not. It helps if you are a place with vistas or have some other prettiness to you.

The word ecology is attributed to the German biologist and naturalist and bestselling author Ernst Heinrich Philipp August Haeckel and first appeared in his book *Generelle Morphologie der Organismen,* published in 1866. It is written that more people learned of evolutionary theory prior to World War I through his prodigious publications than any other source. Haeckel coined (language=currency) numerous terms still in use, stem cell and phyllum among them.

Ecology combines the Greek word for dwelling or house or dwelling place with the general suffix for word or language; the house or dwelling place, of course, is also known as Earth. I wonder what Darwin and his peers would think of the fine mess we have made of the Great Dwelling place with our little fires and our taste for machines that kick out fumes, how distraught they might be to see what great data we have access to and what little use it is in the larger political context of these times.

At any rate, it is time to walk Ecology Trail. I put away my thermos and watch as a woman with dyed, blood-red hair stands precariously on the stone wall and snaps a selfie. There's a thin man in a beat-up leather jacket with an old film camera and he sits on a bench and fiddles with the film, making it look harder to load film than it is in reality. There's a clear view of Alcatraz and the ferries and tour boats that patrol the bay and the absurd, rectangular-solid container ships. These vessels heave and lumber in from the Pacific, making their way towards Port of Oakland cranes, the ones that inspired the *Star*

Wars AT-AT Walkers. Their contents will be plucked out and they will be sent back on their way east, often riding high and empty on the water. On a clear day, you can see Mount Diablo, a modest 3,848 feet, and offering a more expansive view of the Earth's surface than anywhere else on the planet except Mount Kilimanjaro. I clamber down widely spaced earthen stairs and make a sharp left turn.

Bees zizz about, hold position, swoop. There are sixty-four identified bee species in the Presidio, including the nonnative honey bee. Many of the Presidio species are solitary individuals who make nests in the ground. The hive, it turns out, is not a dwelling for all bees, it is the dwelling of the honey bee. The sand draws in water, including from the abundant fog—bees like a moist environment—and makes for a snug home… and so the bees of the Presidio thrive.

It is comforting to see how bees in the Presidio confront their own ecology—having grown up in the suburbs where bees were associated with attacks often launched from fetid summer trash barrels at the community pool, in those contrived suburban swim clubs, in the keystone ecology of matching-house developments with bland concocted names like Mill Creek Town or Flower Valley or Norbeck Meadows. Now, it is a world where many acknowledge much of nature's complexity and diversity is going away, never to return in our lifetimes. It is a relatively new perspective for us humans to articulate, after all these years. This is not because we have not been systematically destroying environments for as long as people have had the wherewithal to do so—but because we simply tried meanwhile to treat nature as an idyll. In my own youth in the so-called country, I was directed to spend my summer time in a cement-lined hole known as the community pool, water saturated with eye-stinging chlorine. The only way to relieve it was to fill the bathroom basin with tap water and open my eyes to wash the chemical out.

Ecology Trail heads north and west, down and into the Monterey pine and cypress and redwoods. Before the trees, though, there is the patch of otherworldly ecosystem created by the shiny green rock called serpentinite that is well worth the time to admire and contemplate.

This lump of slick rock represents a specific moment of success in the Presidio, something that the Presidio is quite good at: allowing indigenous species the time and space to live. Being proximate to this site, fenced off to stop boots and paws from trampling the wee plants, there is a particular feeling for which I have no word, where everything that lives or has lived works in tandem to be alive. While much of the Bay Area has been overrun by Mediterranean plants that hail from farther afield and find the local weather and soil quite to their liking, our fragile, eccentric locals have struggled. Thus, on Ecology Trail it is a scene of survival.

Serpentinite is a toxic rock—pressed up and through the Earth's crust; this ancient oceanic crust dots the Bay Area, surfaced by activity along the San Andreas and Hayward faults. There are peculiarities and mysteries to this mineral that make it a particular favorite of mine. Research indicates that it picks up water as it makes its way from inside the Earth to the surface, gaining buoyancy as it rises. It is described as *floating upward,* pressed up by the denser rock around it. The green color comes from antigorite, a high-temperature serpentine mineral that forms only when the temperature is above 500 degrees fahrenheit.

Along Ecology Trail, a dusky jade shoulder of serpentinite with its mantle of foul soil is home to clarkia and manzanita, two endangered species that have adapted to serpentinite's inhospitable chemistry—heavy on magnesium, chromium, and nickel and low on nitrogen and other essential nutrients for most life. Because of their adaptation, clarkia and manzanita do not have a difficult time growing in this penurious soil. I was told ten percent of California's indigenous flora are restricted to the one percent of California that is covered by toxic soil. Of these plants, a few species evolved in San Francisco—true locals: *franciscan manzanita arctostaphylos hookeri franciscana; Presidio manzanita, arctostaphylos hookeri ravenii; Presidio clarkia, clarkia francisana.*

So. Virginia Woolf wrote in "Street Haunting," an essay about wandering and looking laced with digressions and one I never tire of reading or teaching: "The eye is not a miner, not a diver, not a seeker after buried treasure. It floats us smoothly down a stream; resting, pausing, the brain sleeps perhaps as it looks."

A two-mile stroll down Ecology Trail to the Main Post, a large rectangle of rather dull but useful lawn grass, a place where over priced food trucks (a twenty buys you pizza and a plastic cup of rosé from a spigot) and families gather on summer nights in the Presidio. The Main Parade Ground is

View from Ecology Trail back to Spire

lined by orange-brick buildings, which are home to tourist-beckoning concerns. There is no reason for anyone who lives in the Presidio to come to the Main Parade Ground to trade. It gives the space a feeling akin to the Mall in Washington, DC, lined with Smithsonians. We have no Smithsonian in the Presidio. We have The Walt Disney Family Museum, which is a surprisingly apt fit in terms of its exhibitions. How so? Perhaps there is an argument that it was Walt Disney, more than Thoreau or Muir, who *defined nature* for many of us. I came to this thought one afternoon while wandering a show of Mary Blair's work. Blair was a key artist and lone woman among the Disney animation team, and she gave faces to Peter Pan and Alice in Wonderland. What was her inspiration? From the show it was unclear—however, there were references to the whole lot of them downing martinis at lunch. This could explain a few things. But. What I started thinking about was how these movies impressed on me a specific feeling for the forest, as well as a color sense of nature; one that was understandable even in its indeterminacy.

Crissy Field

I clambered on the round-the-park shuttle and moved myself to the northerly fringe of the Park, Crissy Field. The Presidio is a joint jurisdiction space between the Presidio Trust and the National Park Service, and Crissy is Park Service terrain. I walked along the sandy path called the Golden Gate Promenade that runs from the Warming Hut Café and shop to the St. Francis Yacht Club on the eastern end, past a string of hillocks and tidal lakes. More than 100 species of birds can be seen over the course of the year in and around the marshy area. Migratory birds stop over here as they travel the Pacific Flyway, hang out with permanent avian residents.

The marshes were always the locus of dumping and despoiling from the earliest days of human habitation and were slowly filled with rubbish and then they were built on and then the concrete came. When they were restored, a reported forty acres of concrete was removed.

The airfield had emerged following the Panama-Pacific International Exposition of 1915 and was in use from 1919 to 1936. Grainy black-and-white photos show early airmen preparing to take off from a rutted grass strip alongside a windy bay in an open-air biplane.

It has been stunning over the years to watch the land come back to life. The restoration was formally completed in 2001 and in the last decade of walks, I have felt the place re-establish itself as place rather than built thing. The tidal marsh has settled into place and the egrets pick their way along amongst the shags and gulls.

I attended a talk where the topic was how to design this mile-and-a-half strip of land, and the care that was given to restoration and rest—how benches or picnic tables are strategically sprinkled along the wide, sandy path. This was a key project for bringing the Presidio into the mind of the people. It was the first large restoration project, and the goals included showing how vital the Presidio could be for *re-creation*—a term I adore, the idea that when we are outside we re-create ourselves. There was toxic soil to remove and the tidal marsh to reimagine and rebuild. There was tension between the historic preservationists (airfield) and the native habitat restorers. In the end, we got both. The flat, mushy stretch of grass once called airfield and the revived lagoon.

The space is also imagined as a place to show art and for a time the *Cool Globes* exhibit lined the promenade, in response to the Clinton Global Initiative. I liked to bring my art and design students down to Crissy, to get them out of the classroom, and the globes were a good excuse to get outside. The founder of the project was quoted on the website as never having felt she was an environmentalist, instead associating that term with people in inflatable boats, bouncing on the Pacific, trying to protect the whales. When one student read that aloud to the class, someone else said, *hey, didn't you used to go to sea with Greenpeace? Are you an environmentalist?* This question made me feel old like I had been with Thor Heyerdahl on the *Kon-Tiki* and I almost mentioned Heyerdahl but stopped myself: Thinking of this reference made me feel old, too.

The *Cool Globes* are scaled like industrial washing machines, each individually decorated by a group or individual artist to reflect a concern about climate change and pollution. Because of this theme, some of the globes were strikingly ugly. All together, assembled like a rotund army of ideas, they made a particular effect. Text blocks explained the globes and other projects were in place to make sure a fresh generation become bold leaders for thriving parks, healthy communities, and a more environmentally just society.

It is said that ethnographers decide what becomes an ethnographic object—memory prompts that line museum shelves the world over, those bits of old tins, grass from huts, rusty spurs—and thus define what we remember. They capture an environment, a story, a particular place. Some of the globes were made to look like our Earth. Some used the globe as a structure on which to hang objects, plastic tubing, metal, other industrial bits, a sort of bricolage. My students and I stopped and had sandwiches and talked about how much fuel it had taken to ship the globes all over the world. They became heated in their opinions. I stopped chewing my cheese sandwich and said, mouth half full, *now you are being environmentalists. Welcome.*

As to the conversation about who is and who isn't an environmentalist, I thought of how it's all about degrees—a game of inches, really. The Wardian case exemplifies my thinking on the topic: named for Nathaniel Bagshaw Ward, a physician with a passion for botany. Dr. Ward was a person of his times—he created his first Wardian case in the early nineteenth century, a time when London was lost in a cloud of foul air. Air so foul outdoor plants collapsed and died. So Dr. Ward decided, as the story goes, to make a small glass case for his beloved ferns. In these safe havens, ferns breathed afresh. Were these ferns in their glass vitrines yet wild? Yes. Was Ward an environmentalist?

I think of the wild and what comes to mind: *Refuge. Get away from it all. Silence the madding world.* I guess for some there are ideas of the world as a giant gym, a place for climbing things and sliding on snow and big fires roasting trout pulled painstakingly from the river via a series of intricate flies. I think of the wild and how it inhabits urban spaces, as image, memory, park, as a place for art to show ideas of our larger situation. Are city parks actually wild places? It depends on whom you ask. Ask someone who spends the summer hiking the Sierras, and you hear *no.* Ask someone who lives in Antarctica how wild they think the western Sierras are today, and they say *not really.* Ask someone who spends all her time walking around the Presidio, picking up bits of euc blossoms and chewing on them, and she will whisper, *yes.*

I walk along Crissy Field. A camera recently installed at East Beach peers down at us. Wild?

The camera is enlisted on days when my body refuses to hit the trails or the flat-grey rain sky beats down hard from the northwest. On those days, I can use my touchpad to move the

electronic eye over the trail, down to Fort Point, back to the
lagoon, east to the cemetery, west across the water to Fort Baker.
The camera is new, and so most days there is no one to compete
with me for use—although sometimes they make us queue.

I point out the camera. The students love the camera, they
take pictures of the camera.

The narrow beach and water are crowded with men and
women in wetsuits, launching into the air with boards and sails.

I find this theater to be unbeatable, a marvel to watch. How
strong their arms must be: Why don't their arms pull right out
of their sockets? How can the wind not rip their arms off their
bodies? Impossible to comprehend. How free from fear they
are, like those early airmen catapulting into the sky from the
grass field. These people in black wet suits, hurtling across the
waves, whipping up towards the sky. I would be so terrified—I
would be terrified that I would be swept out to sea, swallowed
by sharks.

Every once in a while something goes bad for these kite
sailors and they find them clinging to buoys over by San
Quentin. It is still winter and so the hills are still green. So
the colors of this view layer out this way, light jade of water,
the slash of garish neon kites, the shiny black suits, the orange
oxide bridge, the pale ochre buildings across the water, deeper
blue-greens of cypress and pine trees, viridian hills, alizarin
crimson details japped in.

At home, in the afternoon, I sit on the carpet with my
daughter, who is eight, and we look at a geology textbook,
from an undergraduate geology course I took while a graduate
student at Iowa. I was that student who arrived early, sat in the
front row, and raised my hand a lot. The book offers a solid
understanding of what continents are made from and how
they slide around as part of the tectonic plate system. I turn
to North America, and we see how the rock underlying the
Presidio is 100- to 200-million years old. My daughter flips
ahead in the book while my son curls up with his Game Boy,

the hand-held game machine. Many mothers fear or shun the Game Boy, but not me. I find it fascinating. I am envious of how much he enjoys it.

She reads aloud from the text, part of a school assignment, and takes notes on the illustrations. These are cross sections of the West Coast of North America 100 million years ago. I look at the drawings. The ocean's crust slips like a serpent under the continent, and pillow basalts, chert, and limestone-capped seamounts were scraped off, and serpentinite formed at the upper mantle to create the Franciscan complex.

My daughter asked, *Is that why we call the city San Francisco?*

Um, no, I answer. *The city is named for Saint Francis of Assisi, an Italian Catholic saint.*

Then I tell her about Saint Francis, and how he wanted us to all be really close to nature, how he talked to the birds near the town of Bevagna, how he persuaded a wolf to stop menacing a town, how he wanted us all to slow down and stop buying things and listen to the world and embrace all of its beauty. She asked if she could include him in her science report and I said, *Why not?*

We live in post-disciplinary times, I believe, and Saint Francis was ahead of his time in many ways—and ahead of ours in many ways. Later that night, when I tuck in the children, who share a room with bunkbeds, I pull out a set of cards, the size of playing cards, which I had purchased in Assisi, each one a photo showing a scene inspired by Saint Francis' famed "Canticle of the Creatures." I explained how it was also called "The Canticle of Brother Sun" and read some of the work. They listened, rapt, trying to imagine what the world was like in 1255 when he penned these ideas: Praised be You, my Lord, through our Sister Mother Earth, who sustains and governs us, and who produces various fruit with colored flowers and herbs. We looked at the cards together and my daughter practiced her reading. The photos are in color and showed the Italian countryside. She picked her favorite and read: Praise be to Thee My Lord, for air and clouds, clear sky and all the weathers.

When I turned off their lamp, the orange halogen glow of the street lamp filtered into the room. It is very quiet in the Presidio at night, very still. Many roads and neighborhoods are either unlit or partially lit to keep the habitat dark for nocturnal residents, the owls, the skunks, and the writers. I wished them both a good night, and we all told each other how much we loved one another.

I immediately retreated to my Steelcase desk and fished around in the deep drawer that holds 20 years of notebooks. Each of these was a moment of hope and inspiration and represents different moments in my life in their very form: The years of invoking Bruce Chatwin by using only Moleskines and then the years I stopped using Moleskines because they became part of the hipster armature; the notebooks purchased when I lived in Thailand and reported the news, when I was rapt with Japanese misspellings and malaprops on plastic-covered notebooks featuring large-eyed animals; the years of wanting all the notebooks to be green and bright and cheerful; the years of the oversized black sketchbook, under the hopeful umbrella called I will not only write long books but also illustrate them beautifully, too.

I pulled out one of the Italian notebooks, brown kraft-paper cover, and flipped through black-and-white photos of Assisi I had shot with my Olympus OM-1n. I had been there three times and had tried to write about Saint Francis each time. On the most recent journey, I had travelled to Bevagna, a small picturesque place with a square described by John Ruskin as perhaps the most beautiful square in all of Europe, Ruskin who said *we should learn to draw before we learn to write.*

The Cathedral in nearby Assisi is a very early medieval building and I had made a point of driving there each morning from Bevagna, arriving ahead of the tour buses, walking its narrow streets, stopping for an espresso, then heading for the Cathedral to study it in detail. I had been captivated by the entwined symbols of both the serene and the horrible in its design, one view of lovely vines and another of terrifying monsters biting each other's necks.

One morning, as the nave started to fill with tourists from around the world, I asked a compact, well-dressed man at the information desk if he could direct me to a tour. He took me to a group that was starting out, led by a smiling Franciscan priest in brown robes and sandals. I nodded and thanked the man and hurried to catch up with the tour.

As we stopped at a painting of Mary, our guide pointed out that many felt it was *the most beautiful painting of Mary in all of Christendom.* He said this with both certainty and joy, and we all crowded together to get a closer look. As the group admired it, the guide walked around and asked us informally where we were all from.

When I said, *the United States,* he said, *oh, so you are in the Delegation to the Holy See!* It then became clear that this was not an ordinary tour group, but a group of diplomats of some nature. That explained a bit: The slightly stiff manner of dressing, the carefully coiffed hair, the general vibe of understated wealth. I was so startled I could not answer. So I just smiled dumbly. Then he wanted to know how often I had seen the Holy Father. Luckily, he was interrupted by a distinguished man in a red tie and grey suit who said politely we were off schedule. As they walked to another part of the church, I held back and gave them the slip. I wandered around the church alone, thinking about the year 1255 and how much of a contrast this medieval church must have been to anything else anyone had ever seen. How the general aesthetic was mud and hay and how people lived to the ripe old age of fourteen and that was that. I mused how it was easy to be hopeful in my times when things were always developing towards what was sold as an ever-brighter future for humanity, even while the Age of the Anthropocene dawned and we slowly ground down other species with rare skill. I thought about how the Sun and Moon were equally gorgeous now and how we did not talk about them after a certain year of grammar school if we were not physicists or astronomers or poets or painters. I thought how that was a pity and how perhaps there were aspects of the thirteenth century we should try harder to hold on to—rather than allowing those values and human views of the natural world and God to go slipping like so much sand through our fingers.

Driving home to Bevagna in one of those impossibly small cars, with cars moving entirely too fast, on roads entirely too narrow (not everything of the thirteenth century should be maintained), I decided to stop at the field where Saint Francis preached to the birds. I have always loved this story of how a man from a middle-class family, Giovanni di Pietro di Bernardone, found his life of privilege to be somehow off the mark, how one day in a church called San Damiano the Christ on the Cross spoke to him, and how over time he became what the bureaucratic hierarchy considered to be a dangerous radical. This was one reason, I have read, he was consigned to the back yard bird bath: It was a way to gently dismiss his vision of a world where all species lived as one in celebration of the glory of God.

Over his life Francis became so close to animals that he could converse with them, and I have always accepted these conversations as a form of fact, not as metaphor—that is, I don't care if the conversations looked like those imagined by Disney animators. There are ways beyond words to engage with other species. There is the story of how he was able to talk a wolf out of terrifying the hill town of Gubbio. As I drove, I thought about a painting by Giotto in the Basilica of Saint Francis of Assisi. It is a marvelous fresco, the pale silvery greens of the paint perfectly capturing the muted colors of the Italian countryside, the olive trees, grasses, the stonework; he is leaning towards the birds assembled on the ground, under a large tree.

There is a small shrine marking this avian conversation. I stop my car at the site, a brick wall with a painting of Francis, framed by carved birds. There are fresh flowers in clear and green glass vases left at the monument. I wonder who brings the cut flowers, and who has assembled the yellow flowers planted in pots wrapped in yellow paper. I wonder who refills the candleholders hanging from chains and who decided to enclose the monument with a low metal fence. Francis had seen many birds gathered and had preached to them—in what is marked as the beginning of his unique relationship with animals as a subject and subjects for his preaching. In his preaching to the birds, he asked them to be aware that God had given them feathers for clothes and wings to fly and all the other things they needed. I liked how he noted that God had made them noble among species, how he had given them life in the thin, pure air.

The memorial itself left me cold. Perhaps the contrast to the basilica and Giotto? Or to the square in Bevagna? I left the site and walked into the nearby field, stopping to watch three crows and two doves gliding in the pale-blue sky. On the distant hill, Assisi rose.

That evening, in the pale light of dusk, I sat in the small square at Bevagna with my notebooks and a glass of Rosso di Montefalco, a renowned Umbrian red wine, and tried to write about Saint Francis and the birds. No, I realized, there are some stories that are simply told by a place—if you want to know Francis you need to either look at the paintings of Assisi and the man or you need to find photos of the place or you need to get there, which is not entirely realistic but still to me feels like fact. The words and the actions of his life are best felt and seen in the frescos and in the air around Assisi. I closed my notebook, put the cap back on my fountain pen, and sat back. In a stone building overlooking the square, upstairs, windows thrown open, I could see a Korean woman and an older Italian man. He was teaching her to sing operas and her voice, thin but confident, filled the air.

NOTEBOOK TWO

Are cities just wild places buried under our little schemes to dig, build, shovel, jack hammer? Soon enough, nature will surge back. This gives me comfort. It always surges back in some new form or other. I think about those Roman aqueducts in the South of France and you know those Romans never thought their work would be the stuff of landscape painters and school kids on overseas adventures. Are cities basically sitting ducks, waiting for their original use to fade and then for the next round of decay and pillaging? I saw a quote from a sculptor who works in sand and concrete, noting that when the inevitable apocalypse descends, the first art to go will be those of the artists who worked in steel and bronze. They will be melted down first. Therefore he worked in less valuable materials. Strategy.

Why is looking at a bay enough for some? Why do others need to represent it? The water today a pale shade of jade green. The sky grey. Against these cool tones, that bridge an impossible shade of mischievous orange brown.

While the name *Presidio* states a fact of use, a fort, a garrison, here is where we arm ourselves and prepare for the worst, the Presidio has always been more about place than soldiers or war—even to the men, long ago, who were the principal landscape and building designers, Army officers and government employees. They saw this place was more than all that cannon emplacement and cheap housing routine.

They saw that while the Presidio might be defined equally by its isolation from the city itself, its otherness of shores and messy forests—it could also be a performance of other ideas, a place of architecture. Fort Scott was a dream by a man who felt the site was too perfect to be ruined by Army-ugly building schemes. And he told a story that people heard and so Fort Winfield Scott was designed and built.

Baker Beach is also where the first Burning Man lit up the night sky—when, in 1986, to mark the summer solstice, two men built an eight-foot-tall wooden man and twenty people watched as it burned.

Now when thousands of people head out annually to the desert for the event and spectacle called Burning Man, I like to remember it was the fact of this one urban wild beach, pounded by horrific waves in winter and packed with families on hot days, that gestated a singular, transformative spectacle of art, bodies, and structures.

EPISODE THREE

64 degrees F; wind from the south at 7 mph, cloudy. No surf of any note, waves press towards the beach with the gentle tremble that says, lake. Huge coils of sea vegetables tangle with the water, bulbs built as flotation devices, the color of oxidized bronze.

March: On Slug Trails

I walk down to Baker Beach on a steep path, through mixed cypress and eucalyptus forest, dart across the road to avoid trucks and cars whose drivers are

View looking northwest from the Presidio

entranced with the ocean view, eyes off the road—then into a thicket of recovering dune scrub awash with lemon flowers and abuzz with some of the five dozen or so bee species that call this place home. From here, the trail opens up across a steep stretch of dune, a Busby Berkeley-style entrance to the grandest theater of ocean on the planet, the Pacific. And on this day, the Pacific *is pacific,* water placid and azure, a seasonal invitation to come wrap yourself in the mottled cinnamon-flecked foam or lounge on the sea-glass strewn beach.

At sea level, all conspires to form a perfect frame for orange oxide and engineering design, a statement of place up there with Stonehenge and Tour d'Eiffel and more recently Kapoor's bean. The Golden Gate Bridge stretches out a half mile or so from the north end of the beach, taupe rocks and massive grey dunes. Baker Beach is often the backdrop in advertisements and films, a view of water and bridge with nary a building nor car in sight.

The surf gently rolls towards the shore. It is empty save the professional dog walkers and me. They are a caste unto themselves in San Francisco and the Presidio, where they ply their trade with particular vigor: Men and women who hire out themselves to walk dogs that would otherwise be trapped in homes and apartments all day. There are more dogs in San Francisco than children.

The dog walkers talk in loud voices. *Charlie, I told you to stay with the other dogs, you are the new dog. Elias, please get your ball. Ginger, heel.* They carry plastic sticks, slightly bowed, used to catapult tennis balls down the beach, for those dogs inclined towards this exercise.

Some lands are hilly and rock-strewn and catch the light in such a particular pattern they seem forever ready for the eye. Some are sloping and enmeshed in growing things, obliterating edges, rejecting light and contrast, places with no beginning and no end. It is in such a land where I walk.

Lost in these observations, I almost stumbled on a dead bird. Poor cormorant! Yellow tongue hanging out, beak cocked open. Brown feet turned in, clawish crone hands attached to a penguin body. I see no evidence of a wound and wonder how this fellow died. Simply end of time on Earth, end of game, time to die? I wonder when the bird made its last flight, how it felt as the flight became too tough, recalling how birds fly because they have to do so to survive predation and to find food. When birds live in an environment where flight is not necessary to survival, like the New Zealand islands before man and the Antarctic today, they walk around on land and swim. Flight takes a great deal of energy and comes with an array of hazards, the simple physics of being a small, lightweight object in motion in a tumultuous sky.

Stones, great mounds of deep grey, shoved across the sand by the sea's rough hand. It is what we love about the sea, how alternately rude and gentle is its touch. I once dated a man who disagreed with my instinct to sift through sand, shards of sand dollars, fragments of granite, rounded grey stones, shells opalescent, grey knobs of wood, whittled smooth by water. I left that man one day, and I believe the main reason centered on not wanting to hear his voice saying, Put that down. Leave it here where it's supposed to be.

When you are on the beach, the activity of the sky foregrounds. Land recedes. Sitting or walking on this edge is as close to life as a bird as we will ever know. Here the shore birds of the near Pacific ply their trade, running, diving, standing in patient meditation, gazing to the west.

The maritime layer is quickly overtaking it all, first the horizon, then it obscures the Golden Gate Bridge, the hills of Marin, tells me it is time to stomp back up the sand ladder to the forest. As I climb the log ladder laid down over sand, the sky moves in a gesture of embrace. *come to me,* it says, *all you fog-bound beach walkers, let me wrap you in my hair.*

At home, I find a banana slug curled into a c on the wet concrete by my door. I crouch on the concrete. Stems rising from the slug's head in a perfect V, pressing its light-sensing cells towards my outstretched finger. The slug turns. Mustard-color back hunches. I take a piece of bark and gently lift the slug, then place into camouflaging ice plant. Slugs get squished on concrete walks by people hurrying off to work, coffee in hand. *Not today,* I say to the slug. *That will not be your fate today.*

Later that morning, I walk into the San Francisco Museum of Modern Art. A Matisse show is in place and I engage in a perverse pleasure: listening to the audio tour of the art. Curators love to do this, to guide and direct our experiences, beyond all the guidance and direction inherent in a show itself, an act that states, we know what art is, and we know when it was made and where it ought to hang on this wall. Don't get me wrong, I love museums and curators. But. I walk the exhibition, listening to a man telling me how Matisse was more interested in form than story.

Isn't form a story, too, I whisper to the disembodied voice. He doesn't answer me. *Isn't form study the same work to pursue truth?*

Downstairs the artist Ann Hamilton made stacks of indigo shirts. Laborers not represented in history being a rough summary of the story. Tall mounds of blue denim, like a Levis' supply house. A woman sits at a desk, erasing. Someone says to someone else, hey, come here, she is erasing stuff from a book. I watch. The book is a government text on land and water use. The woman erasing has brown hair and sits a wooden table, acting like she is all alone with her task.

My companion, a man who deals in financial transactions by day and skis the Sierras by weekend, scrunches his handsome face, and questions it all. *I don't understand what she is doing. How does the book relate to the shirts? It makes my brain hurt. I preferred just shirts. Why doesn't she sew? Or rip out seams? Why erasing?*

I stop and hold his rough hand. In the world where he does business, people get put onto "plans" for ninety days before they are fired. Once most of them go on a "plan" they know they are going to be fired. But the state requires a performance plan, some sense these people are being helped, and not simply drummed out the door. But in most cases, they are being drummed out the door. They know it. The company knows it. It's all a performance, very much, in my mind, like the stacked shirts and the books being erased. I hold my tongue.

It's not the sort of art we learn about at school, or that we see in many museums. It is a harder landscape this art, art that asks you to relax the brain and let the connections happen. It is art that maybe cannot be summarized into ideas such as *this person is more interested in line than narrative.* There is no audio tour for this show.

Fifty-six degrees and foggy. Another banana slug on the cement walk. The ocean erased by the sky. Thick white fog, low visibility, braying, mooing, crying out foghorns. This banana slug is five to six inches in length, moving towards ice plants on its own, seeking cover. Moving with the same steady motion of a hand pulling a needle through fine fabric. One steady draw.

Once again, I squat down and extend my finger and the slug peers at it. I remain absolutely still, and the slug changes course and moves towards me. It begins to make my acquaintance. I know to make no sudden moves. No teetering on heels or all congress with this slug will immediately vanish as stems retract into head, and slug scrunches into a ball.

The banana slug is the state mollusk of California. I don't know how many states appoint state mollusks. It is a fact that does not appeal to me, this owning of species as political symbol: *State flower, state rock, state poet laureate.*

Exhausted from a day of art and walking, I stretch out on my orange sofa and sleep. I dream, a vivid cinema: *The red-tail hawk that nests in the cypress trees behind my home snared by a small boy with a crew cut. He keeps the hawk's head in water and begins to ready his killing tools, a knife. First, he decides to blind the bird. I watch from small scrub, and approach the boy. I talk him into letting the bird go, even though the boy is set on showing his father how he, too, can trap an animal. I untie the bird and wrap it in a towel. The hawk shivers and cries. The hawk sleeps for many hours, fading into days. I check to see it is alive. When it awakens, there will be food to gather, moles, mice, some other small ground animal. I wonder how hard these will be to catch.* The wind startles me awake. I look around, groggy. Then relief: There is no injured bird at my side.

In the early morning, in the gloamy light, before the sun reaches its ultra-white ascendency over the eastern rise, I find myself often in the company of the banana slug. My slug memories from childhood embarrass me now. They were a source of summer entertainment in the woods of Maryland, and I used to enjoy dumping salt on them. What a horrible way to die, I have since learned. Dehydration a slow, torturous demise.

I walk the concrete sidewalk strewn with eucalyptus leaves and stop to observe an unusually large band of banana slugs— five in all. The slugs crazed, meandering paths are laid out in so much goo. The slug trail and trial on concrete suggests Jackson Pollock, one of the paintings where the eye is invited to wander curvilinear paths, a line offering neither destination nor point of embarkation.

I squat on the ground. One banana slug, more ochre than yellow, perhaps five inches in length is ambling along, ignoring the cluster of colleagues; I presume it has been meandering amidst the leaves for some time. No one knows how long these slugs live in the wild, although they clock in for a couple years in man-made habitats.

The slug's slimy path shines, a varnished trail easier to follow than Hansel's, should any other living creature desire to follow its meanderings. The slug must have been on a single three-foot square of concrete for some time, the artful lines jam and loop together.

When not patrolling the woods with the slugs, work takes me, via words and images, deeply into other people's experiences and creations. Not long ago, sitting in my white office, surrounded by, in no particular order, Antarctic rocks, a Playmobil polar explorer, my stapler collection, an album featuring Frank Sinatra smoking in a yellow sweater (hints of banana slug), and a pink ceramic bowl with white ceramic milk bouncing aloft (student project, this one investigating the iconography of breakfast cereal boxes), I happened on one George Evelyn Hutchinson, the father of modern limnology, the scientific study of lakes and other fresh water bodies of water.

My day job means working with architects, interaction, industrial, graphic, sound, and light designers, among others. Many are also writers. We gather at an art school housed in a re-imagined former Greyhound bus garage and try to help students make things. What sorts of things? Hard to explain in brief, but one for instance is adapting mobile technologies to guide inquiries; for instance way finding, mapping, and the lay of the land in general are topics of considerable scrutiny in our halls. We explore the unknown via ubiquitous computing and the iterations and discussions make the head swim.

My mid-day break is a meander out of this goo into some hard, cold reality. My escape hatch for half an hour or so each day often old-timey science and history books. I collect them from resellers, some online, some during wanders of used bookstores. I always buy more than I can read and I always love what I buy for all sorts of reasons too complicated and personal to detail here.

I like the look and feel and smell of the books, the attention to end papers, the deep-blue fabric covers and bindings worn to grey at corners, the embossed golden titles. I like reading about people who have done brave things around ecosystems and landscapes. I like people who fight to save the world. Door closed, iPhone off. Thirty minutes of stories before I hit the trenches again.

Back to Hutchinson. In 1933, while in Reno, Nevada, (for a mere six weeks to get a divorce from his first wife), he advanced ideas on physical and chemical conditions, with calculations on heat budgets, oxygen deficits, and a new approach to the stability of meromictic lakes.

Meromictic lakes are a particular curiosity; because they lack complete water circulation, the deepest water contains no dissolved oxygen, the sediments are relatively undisturbed and therefore offer a detailed record of the history of the lake. This is water behaving like rock: permanently stratified. In holomictic lakes (also called "ordinary lakes"), surface and deep water physically mix, often driven by wind, wind driving waves across the lake's surface.

Hutchinson coined the term *meromictic* in 1957 in his *Treatise on Limnology.* Very little can live in the deep recesses of the meromictic lake, although it is interesting to note one of them is a bacteria, purple sulfur.

A meromictic lake in action, August 12, 1986: Lake Nyos in Cameroon, shaken up by winds or heavy rains or a landslide—no one knows for certain—unleashed a limnic eruption, also called an exploding lake, a rare sort of natural disaster. Imagine the placid, deep blue undisturbed waters of Lake Nyos, 1.5 square kilometers and 200 meters deep.

Imagine that day. How people gazed at the lake's wide, blue calm, thought of their youth, wondered what sort of weather lay before them. Maybe someone held a metal cup filled with sweet tea. The lake intact in a piece of volcanic landscape called Oku, inside a maar, in a maar and basaltic cinder-cone landscape. Maars can be pictured easily: circular indentations caused by volcanic eruptions, then filled with water. It is landscape designed to illustrate, otherworldly.

Then, Lake Nyos bubbles awake. The mechanism similar to what happens inside a soda can; only in this case, through volcanic activity or decomposition of organic material, massive amounts of dissolved CO_2 saturate a lake. The water pressure aids in the ready dissolution of the CO_2 and like a soda, bubbles form when pressure is released, like popping the top off a bottle of Coke.

A cloudy mixture of carbon dioxide and water droplets forces itself aloft—those who survive will remember a mythic cloud, a cloud attributed to folklore, the work of an enraged spirit-woman. The cloud, fifty meters thick, takes off like a jet engine, roaring skyward at 100 kilometers an hour; 120 meters above the shoreline within the crater, folding all living things into its mire, then drifting twenty to fifty kilometers downward.

The sleep-offering vapor, swirling into at least four villages, where the people would be discovered, many still in their beds, sleeping into eternity. After the gas was released, Lake Nyos sank a meter lower in surface level; the cloud left at least 1,700 people, as well as thousands of cattle, and birds, dead.

In the 1960s, Hutchinson testified before the Royal Society. He spoke up against a dastardly plan to put a military base on Aldabra Island in the Indian Ocean, now a UNESCO World Heritage site, part of the Seychelles, a raised coral atoll, the second-largest of its kind in the world, home to the world's largest population of giant tortoises, as well as the Aldabra rail, the largest surviving flightless bird of the Indian Ocean region. He argued abandoning the planned destruction of the complicated biota.

Hutchinson's voice prevailed. "I have not expressed, in the formal document, my personal feelings on the matter, namely that the intended occupation of the island is a sickening and criminal attack on what I would call a natural work of art, and bad as it is in itself, would set precedents that would impoverish the world even more completely and rapidly than is being done. I cannot believe that the people involved wish to go down in history as they well may with the epitaph, 'They saved money.'" One reporter called Hutchinson a sage of enlightenment.

Too soon it is time to go to a meeting to talk about what classes we want to offer when the fall semester begins. Classes change because tools change for making things, and humans need to find new ways to be integrated into these making systems. We are in the midst of a paradigm shift in design. But what has become of the Aldabra rail? Has it continued to thrive in the Seychelles? I decide it is OK to be late for the meeting on the ephemera of technologies and their role in shaping human culture. Instead, I image search "climate change" and "Aldabra" and gaze at the twenty-two islands of Aldabra, centered on a blue lagoon, home to the 100,000 or so tortoises. And of course the flightless rail. I find a drawing of a white-throated rail standing on the back of a tortoise.

When I get to the meeting, one of my colleagues wants to know what delayed me. I tell him a giant tortoise and a flightless bird. He stops a moment and shakes his head, muttering about how weird I am. Then he talks about how students need to do more speculative design work, imagining the future of food. I keep my mouth shut and imagine those tortoises. Where will they go when their land that is eight meters above sea level is swamped by the seas?

The banana slug is part of the mollusk family, *ariolimax columbianus,* and relatives include the delicious oyster, the literary squid, and the pesky snail, all of whom have a place in world cuisines. Banana slugs can grow to be eighteen inches long, although the biggest neighborhood slug appears closer to eight inches. Still and all, a big slug. Slugs disgust most people. Most of us think slug and see traits: slimy, hairless, cold. What if we had to touch it? Their natural condition defines decay: slimy, hairless, cold.

"Do you like slugs?" I asked my son, Will, one afternoon.
"That's a weird question," he said. "There aren't many people who think slugs are amazing and extraordinary," he added with the cool certainty of teenage years.
I suggested this was because of some pure, innate disgust brought on by the collection of features: cold, slimy, and hairless.
"Well, warm, slimy, and hairless seems pretty bad, too," Will noted.

While banana slugs hold me in their thrall, I cannot say they feel the same way about me. I read about them in my free time, and I know they are mollusks with no visible sign of a skeleton. I know they are among the largest mollusks on the planet. I know we believe slugs excrete slime because predators hate slimy food. (Raccoons will eat them in a pinch but only if they can be rolled in dirt first to get rid of the slime.)
But I wonder if their artful meanderings aren't worthy of

closer consideration, a conceptual art moment in the forest, a moment of co-habitation and co-creation. If not for the concrete, there would be no canvas for human eyes, no moment of wonder, alone at daybreak.

When I walk outside at dawn, these trails glow, a muted rainbow spectrum. Maybe, I think, as I try to record the look of the morning's perambulations, this is my purpose in life. Perhaps my life has been designed to see those slug paths and tell the world the story of their glory. Maybe the slugs have summoned me. And now there is work to do. The sun breaks over the trees and the moment is lost. The trails fade to deep grey lines, a neon sign unplugged. I pick my way down the trail to the beach. Banana slugs pick their way across surfaces, faces without eyes, leaving a moist trail as rune. It is in such a land where I walk.

NOTEBOOK THREE

Before it was called San Francisco, this place was called Yerba Buena, *beautiful garden.* I came across Juana Briones, a first-generation Californio, named as one of the three early settlers of the city. Briones lived in the Presidio in the early nineteenth century, in a place called Tennessee Hollow. Stanford University archeologists were excavating the site of her home when we first moved to the Presidio. They found the foundation of the home and also the trash and discards of those days, which included tools used by Native Californians. Briones is lauded as an astute businesswoman who was equally a healer, having learned the art of herbs as remedy from the Native Californians. Reading about her trials I am stunned by the depth of her perseverance—she had eleven children and still had time to found Yerba Buena, heal sick sailors with her herbal remedies, all the while being horribly abused by a dreadful husband. Briones petitioned for ecclesiastical separation from her husband. According to the Stanford site capturing the excavation, she was unable to read or write and her petition was transcribed by one of the priests at Mission Santa Clara. In her petition, she wrote,

". . . I do not fear to shoulder the conjugal cross that the Lord my Father and my Mother the Holy Church have asked me to bear, being in a state that I have freely chosen. What I truly fear is the loss of my own soul forever, and what is more, I fear the destruction of my unfortunate family due to the scandal and bad example of a man who has forgotten God and his own soul, whose only concern is drunkenness and all the vices that come with it, and who no longer cares about feeding his family, a burden that I alone carry with the labor of my own hands, a fact that I can prove with testimonials of exceptional strength if necessary."

The research about the Briones sisters (there were three) continues to unearth ideas about a world perhaps markedly different than the official, recorded history describes. In this scholarship, a picture of life outside of the borders of military-status, patriarchal mode, one where people of varied racial backgrounds and ethnicities were able to find a degree of freedom to acquire land and create their own economic stability. The Briones family, as observed in their buried household waste—what is listed as imported pieces of British white ware, local ceramics, animal bone, and tools used by Native peoples—appear to have engaged in ethnic pluralism.

Water a thin band of opal at the horizon, all else perfectly matte, flat grey. The best thing about grey is green, brown, cerulean, azure, alizarin crimson look so fine against it. What would we do without grey. I celebrate the grey, sing a song of grey. All grey lacks is my ability to imagine its many possibilities.

Grey is a good color for walking. Under this sort of uncertain sky, ideas can float, tether, unmoor. Float again.

We were out in force today after a week of pounding by diagonal rains, dousing cold, creating mud-laden flash-creeks and now a carpet of soil covers the walk.

As the rain abated, my son Will and I darted out to Cal-Mart to stock up on some provisions. Cal-Mart: A San Francisco institution, more so even than Rice-a-Roni and cable cars and whatever else outsiders think of when they muse about "Frisco"—a town of the imagination, not of fact, a town designed for views by the rocks and for fun by successive generations of human inhabitants. Fun is a trite word but that's what we have on our hands now, a waterfront built for visitors, shipping long gone, an economy based on tourism and a grocery store on California Street, sandwiched between Jordan Park and Presidio Heights, down the street from where my children were born, a last-man-standing in a line of shops and restaurants that also were San Francisco institutions until they were not—Young Man's Fancy, Mrs. Brown's Feedbag.

In the checkout line, we talked to Ed, the same man who has been helping us since Will was a tiny baby. Then Ed was the delivery man and would bring our groceries to us in cardboard boxes. Cal-Mart is the sort of old-timey market where things like this persist, the personal credit account with a three-digit number, where you call them on the phone and tell them what you want and they shop for you and then truck it over.

However those were in the days when Will and I lived in a large apartment. Those were the days before we became part of a long-running experiment in living in a small space. I used to write "extremely small space" but over time decided that confused even me—it sounded like we lived in a 300-square-foot box, sharing a single plastic bowl of hot grains for dinner.

I never tire of reading this passage, wherein Major Jones tells us "the main idea:" "The main idea is, to crown the ridges, border the boundary fences, and cover the areas of sand and marsh waste with a forest that will generally seem continuous, and thus appear immensely larger than it really is. By leaving the valleys uncovered or with a scattering of fringe of trees along the streams, the contrast of height will be strengthened . . . In order to make the contrast from the city seem as great as possible, and indirectly accentuate the power of Government, I have surrounded all the entrances with dense masses of wood."—Major William A. Jones, 1883

1886: SF Chronicle reports first mass planting in Presidio on SE slope of Main Post, in the vicinity of Lovers' Lane. Boy Scouts lend a hand.

1895: Army complains trees interfere with drill service.

Early twenty-first century: Tennessee Hollow Watershed Archeological Project declares: "The Presidio is a beautiful park-like area of 1,542 acres . . . the most strategic base on the Pacific, but so badly fortified that an enemy force could take San Francisco almost without a battle."—San Francisco and the Golden Empire, 1935

. . . Shifts in geological formations suggest corresponding micro-environments and indicate that, prior to late 1800s modifications to the area by the U.S. Army, the area was a patchwork of hill slopes, sand dunes, and marshy wetlands with a correspondingly high degree of animal and plant biodiversity.

A list
- **Special status plants**
- **Coast rock cress:** *arabis blepharophylla*
- **Raven's manzanita:** *arctostaphylos hookeri var ravenii*
- **Manzanita is called the mother of all plants.**
- **San Francisco spineflower:** *chorizanthe cuspidata*
- **Franciscan thistle:** *cirsium andrewsii*
- **Presidio clarkia:** *clarkia franciscana*
- **San Francisco Wallflower:** *erysimum franciscana*
- **Dune gilia:** *gilia capitata ssp chamissonis*
- **San Francisco gumplant:** *grindelia hirsutula var. mantima*
- **Marin dwarf flax:** *hesperolinon congettum*
- **Lessingia**
- **San Francisco Campion:** *silene verecunda ssp verecunda*
- **California sea blite:** *suaeda californica*
- **San Francisco owl's clover:** *triphysana floribunda*

The Presidio's vegetation management plan:
Protect and enhance existing native plant communities and their remaining habitat by removing threats to native species, repairing damage to habitat, and increasing reproductive success.

Restore and enlarge nature plant communities by reclaiming habitat from past development, non-native species, and nonnative trees outside of historic forest management zone.

Largest remaining colony of lessingia in San Francisco is at Lobos Dunes near Lobos Creek.

Coyote bush: It is also dioecious, meaning it produces male and female flowers on different plants.

Ansel Adams grew up close to the Presidio and supposedly had his first kiss at Lobos Creek.

Old cash registers—leftover from when the Army was here strewn along Lobos Creek. Bags and bags of trash.

EPISODE FOUR

I become a transparent eye-ball; I am nothing; I see all;
the currents of the Universal Being circulate through me;
I am part or particle of God. —Emerson, Nature

April: On Borders

When I was 12 years old, growing up in then-rural-suburban Maryland, I would return home from a junior high school I hated and watch television, read, or walk in a thin extension of Rock Creek Park. I hated the school for reasons that can be distilled to three factors: open classrooms where teachers were dominated by loud-mouthed, frightening students, often white boys with overcharged Southern accents, boys we called rednecks; the tense results of busing for racial integration that led all of us, black and white, male and female, to take philosophical positions at lunch like, why don't our parents bus their offices out of the blue and leave us out of it; and the absence of books. We never read books. The older kids stole drugs from their parents' medicine chests, did them in gym class, and ambulances were called; and the younger ones smoked in the bathrooms. I have no idea what the adults who ran the school were doing, although I recall some of the teachers smoked pot in their cars during breaks. I was a shy student who dreamed of traveling the world. I did not fit in.

Spending time after school alone was thus an easy choice. If I stayed inside and watched TV in the basement rec room, my mother got upset, wondering about my nonexistent homework. So I left and went for walks in the woods.

I could walk a long way before encountering anything remotely resembling human civilization. One of my more curious compulsions included walking for hours to find what I thought of as "the other side." I knew the woods had to be bounded by roads somewhere and wanted to feel the wide stretch of the place, defined by its end points.

The whole endeavor of seeking a borderline thrilled after a day in that hellish school: Hauling out a stiff backpack, green canvas smelling vaguely musty; grabbing a black knife, with its mysterious blades and miniscule tools; shoving in purloined yellow legal paper and pencil stubs from my father's study— tools for drawing my woods and field notes.

The mid-Atlantic woods taught me refuge through nuance in nature, a creek sunk into its banks, banks a contortion of silvery-umber tree roots and small grey sandy spits, then up to rocky outcrops and slow hills slick with layers of leaves; elms, dogwoods, the occasional tree fort. All alive with fascinators if I took the time to gaze: Spindly water spider skating on black water. There was the tension of coming across the poisonous copper head, a snake that will bite readily and one whose venom can kill you. More likely finds were the blackish berries good for making marks on paper from the bush we called the inkberry or a young dogwood with pale celadon leaves.

I would emerge from the woods in time for a hot dinner with my three sisters and mother, who would sit with us while we ate. My parents never ate with us because my father had to have cocktail time, scotch, first, and my mother had the rest of us on a tight schedule towards being "done" for the night. We were always on a tight budget and dinner was a glass rectangular baking dish with everything assembled and baked into one big hunk, which was cut into sections, like lasagna. These hunks had names, like Laguna Beach Chicken and Mrs. Andrew's Best Pork and Rice. I did not see food ingredients separated at dinner time until a holiday arrived, when the turkey or ham was allowed to stand solo. When my mother would ask what had happened at school that day I would tell her about the horrifying boys who were planning what they called a "race riot" at school the next day and my mother would say, *Oh don't call them rednecks and, no, they're not planning a riot!* And if I tried to add details about what made them rednecks and how they called themselves that and how they furtively sharpened sticks as weapons in art class with tools meant for linoleum block printing, my mother would tell me I was full of bologna, that the teachers would never allow that. Parallel universes: An early education in the fact of experience and the believability of the story. So. I would shut up then, because my mother had already heard and dismissed my report about the art teacher, one of those in smoke-filled cars at lunch, who told us how she let her four-year-old daughter change her name to Pancake Lollypop.

After the meal, I would soak in our peculiar square, pale-blue bath. Easing into the warm water, the day's markings from the woods expeditions made themselves known—legs and arms a Jackson Pollock canvas of scrub, branch, and briar scratches. The acid sting of water on the cuts meant time well spent.

I've never possessed a field botanist's mindset, the focus and drive to consistently record facts of leaf shapes, flowers, to look in order to discover and create a system for recognition or to establish habitat locations. Wouldn't it be a lovely gift now, to have detailed, hand-rendered images of that place, rather fresh and alive in my mind—creek and four seasons, in winter a light crust of pale ice, vanishing in a chaos of summer greens, vines and leaves, reappearing in autumn as leaves died and fell to the ground. To know a place so well from a certain vantage point, in this case my bedroom window: It is something one misses terribly, a particular vantage point of nature quietly at work.

One spring, while I listened to "Good Morning, Starshine" on my new record player, the bulldozers arrived, followed by a squad of dynamiters. That summer, as they felled trees and blasted a new batch of basements into rock and clay, we would sit, my sisters and me, at our white Formica table with a dark brown faux-bentwood frame and eat breakfast cereal. The table shook, panes of glass rattled with each seismic intensity. It all happened so fast. It was all unannounced. I would stand in my front yard in shorts, sweating in the humidity, and wonder.

In weeks, acres of trees and meadows were gone, little springs smashed under soil, wild violets churned into nothing.

Of course this was nothing compared to what was about to come over the next decades. In a few decades this would all be sectioned off and cut into roads, and more houses would pepper the woods, joining the roads named for some fantasy of the American Revolution: George Washington, Cherry Valley, Powder House Drive. As though we were all secret history buffs.

This rural Maryland's future arrived one day in the form of an enormous grocery store, aptly named Super Giant, which sprung up at the crossroads of Route 108 and Georgia Avenue. Awfully big store for such a tiny town, my mother would comment, pulling her sweater closer in the Arctic chill of Giant's summertime air conditioning, and adding, but this area is going to keep growing. The other corners were a black smith, a strip mall, and a meadow. Down the road was a dinner theater and in the other direction a sort-of famous country inn. In the meadows, there were still horses and horse jumps and sometimes a goat or three.

I did not connect the arrival of the Super Giant with the disappearance of woods, so I found its largesse and garish presence thrilling. You could open a popsicle in there and it never melted: No heavy blue sugar water coating fingers, hands, arms. The checkers wore heavy sweaters in summer to stave off a perennial chill. Many checkers were my friends' aunts and mothers. Freezers lined the wide, long aisles, freezers where we could lean in and grab more popsicles—an open-cast mine of the frozen, a gallery of food photography and design—images of waffles brimming with maple syrup, Salisbury steaks in gravy astride tiny corn muffins, tubs of ice cream with elaborate lettering. It was beautiful. So. This was where I also walked, after riding my bike in the blazing heat on soft new-tar roads, fully in the gaze of the wild dogwood, seeking the garish, vulgar cold of the refrigerated store in the Maryland heat.

There was a competition for space going on, one the swallowtails and copperheads would lose, slowly, then more rapidly. Many years later, I returned to Maryland, my parents and sisters and me long since moved away from our home on Powder House Drive, and found an inexplicable maze of roads and turn offs and traffic. I inadvertently drove past the turn off on Georgia Avenue and came upon the old Super Giant, dwarfed by a mini-mall and multiplex theater. There was a drive-up fast food place and gas stations and cars weaving and lunging out of parking lots. What is this place, I asked no one, peering at the jangle of garish signs. Who decided we wanted places to be like this? The stupidity of this thought apparent to me as it floated through my brain. The answer was no one. These places are the result of the insane hive brain of short-sighted capitalism—growth that privileges speed and standardized offerings. Fuck aesthetics, they scream.

I drove by our old house, slowed down. The stand of trees behind the old place was intact with a pink dogwood thriving in the front yard. I eased the car forward and did not look back.

On a chilly April afternoon, I stood on the border of my small back garden, sunk into the dunes above Baker Beach and waited for the maritime layer to wrap me up. This layer: A veil, its own place, an effect that demands careful attention. It teaches a two-dimensional tutorial in perspective, the Z-axis is removed. It is a place where the brain and body are free to float, untethered from distractions like foregrounds, backgrounds, and other permutations of "grounds." The marine layer elicits a feeling of exhilaration and peace in me if only for a moment.

When I am alone, the stories, wild imaginings, and full-on obsessions of explorers have long been the stuff of quiet days or hours. Explorers have a way of explaining their exploits so they make perfect sense. One companion in this aloneness is the American explorer Richard Evelyn Byrd, who was first to fly over the South Pole; he set up Advance Camp about 123 miles from his main base on the Ross Ice Shelf and planned to live there alone, recording the weather and phenomena such as the aurora. This was the 1930s, and Byrd and his men were intuitive, boot-strapping explorers (all Antarctic explorers in those days were boot-strappers, inventors, fix-it pros, dreamers, never-surrender sorts) and perhaps recognizable oddballs in that they were nourished by the idea and fact of ice camps far, far away. Byrd almost died from carbon monoxide poisoning from a malfunctioning heater. He lost sixty pounds before a trio of his team came to save him. (His lead scientist, Thomas Poulter, could hear there was something wrong in Byrd's radio transmissions and bravely led the group that saved his life.) Byrd wrote the book *Alone* about this time and if you have not already delved into it, do so. He came to terms with God and place in those Antarctic days, and it changed him forever. I love the preface: "This book is an account of a personal experience—so personal that for four years I could not bring myself to write it."

In the maritime layer, reminding me of when I lived in Antarctica, my mind meanders to Byrd and then further back to the nineteenth century, to John Cleves Symmes and his Theory of a Hollow Earth. Of all the oddballness of Antarctica, Symmes' theories stand out. I first came upon him while researching my Antarctic book and then, like a new word you see and look up that suddenly appears daily, Symmes' ideas keep poking up in books and essays. His intellectual influence rippled across a young America, an America of the early nineteenth century, an America of transcendentalism, Poe, of Adams and Jackson in the White House, an America not yet wrenched into the deep divides of what was first called the Great War but whose name was changed to the Civil War when there was another, even greater carnage that spread over many lands.

To contextualize Symmes' theories, first cast your mind back to 1692, when the formidable Edmund Halley advanced a theory that Earth is composed of a series of inner concentric spheres capable of sustaining life. Later, Thomas Burnet's *Tellueris theoria sacra,* expanded and revised (The Sacred Theory of Earth) offered complex design ideas for a hollow Earth. Burnet envisioned the planet as a "Mundane Egg," with the shell the Earth's crust and a yolk nestled in the interior. (Burnet's geo-cosmic vision of Earth also is said to function as a kind of microcosmic theory of the psyche.) A Hollow Earth as serious theory is at first impossible to believe; yet Symmes was merely updating and pushing forward an idea of a hollow Earth pondered and written about by esteemed scientists for hundreds of years.

The portals into these worlds existed at the poles. Halley further added operational design: The shells, neatly tucked into each other, were spinning in different directions and were capable of sustaining life. Symmes took up this theory and story, following in the footsteps of scientific giants and spread his ideas through lectures and pamphlets in the early nineteenth century. Symmes. Army officer, trader, and hollow-Earth theorist, namesake of an uncle who had served on the Continental Congress, husband and father, marries a widow with six children and rears them alongside their own. While all of this sounds far-fetched to the modern listener, remember the vellum layer then called the Great Unknown that still covered much of the Earth—indeed it covered more of the planet than the mapped bits. Why not a portal? Why not worlds in worlds? If I type "hollow Earth theory" into Google, I find 235,000 hits in .25 seconds. Among them current discussions of how climate change and melting ice are opportunities to again seek the portals in a freshly ice-free Arctic Ocean.

I read about Symmes' failures as a trader in the then-western outpost of St. Louis, moving to Kentucky with his family and setting to work on his theory of the portals at the ends of the Earth. He hung around a museum in Cincinnati, met John James Audubon (who created a portrait of Symmes) and was apparently hailed (by some) as the "Newton of the West." When he first published his theory, he was widely lampooned in the press as a crackpot. Yet his fervor for the theory of polar portals attracted followers—including James McBride who advanced them by collecting the ideas into an 1826 book, Symmes' Theory of Concentric Spheres. Symmes' had mapped the theory to granular detail, and McBride summarized it: "The Earth is composed of at least five hollow concentric spheres, with spaces between each, an atmosphere surrounding each; and habitable as well upon the concave as the convex surface. Each of these spheres are widely open at the poles. The north polar opening of the sphere we inhabit, is believed to be about 4,000 miles in diameter, the southern about six thousand."

Scientific fact aside, hollow Earth notions offered great material for an emergent style of writing later to be called science fiction: Jules Verne would publish *Journey to the Center of the Earth* in 1864. Edgar Allan Poe would find inspiration in hollow Earth theories for *The Narrative of Arthur Gordon Pym of Nantucket,* a particularly horrifying journey to an imagined South Polar region, filled with cannibals and godlike figures emerging from thick fog.

Symmes then met the newspaper editor and explorer Jeremiah Reynolds, who joined Symmes on the lecture circuit, and they packed houses at fifty cents a ticket, sharing revelations of the Hollow Earth. Reynolds went on to present an idea for an expedition to the US Congress and convinced the legislators to grant him funding. While John Quincy Adams supported these explorations, his successor Andrew Jackson tabled them, so funding was withdrawn. Like all polar obsessives, Reynolds refused to be daunted and privately funded an expedition, which set out for the Antarctic in 1829. Accounts place them on Antarctic shores where they were met with dangerous ice and weather conditions. They turned north, headed back to Valparaiso, Chile, where the crew mutinied and kicked Reynolds off the ship.

The promise of worlds within worlds within worlds yet a creation of the mind and pen to be reopened, two hundred years later, in the early twenty-first century, as the ice at the North Pole slips into memory. Perhaps this is the actual world within a world, that as we reconstruct the Earth's surface with our machines and fires we create worlds of distinct forms that live only as memory, and this world of memory remains a concentric sphere or space within the other one, until the last person who walked it is no more. Then this is subsumed by the new world layer and so we have our concentric, tightly aligned worlds in worlds of the mind.

NOTEBOOK FOUR

Axis Café was the main gathering place for my colleagues at the art and design school. Before it was knocked down to make way for a new development, it was a former something, a former garage of some sort, renovated masonry refurbished and then looking like a trattoria outside of Assisi; enormous glass doors and windows, vine, and plant-festooned walled patio, endless tiny bowls of olives, and tables covered with glasses of sparkling wine. The street was blocked off out front to form a mini park and skaters filmed trick videos and hung out, a few homeless men pitched tents. This bit of park tucked into the city was called Showplace Triangle. When it opened for business on a bright September morning, there was fanfare and talk about repurposing: dumpsters planted with citrus and fig trees, up-ended water pipes holding succulents.

It is part of a movement called Pavement to Parks. I read that twenty-five percent of this seven-mile by seven-mile city named for Saint Francis is now roads and intersections, meaning there are more roads and intersections than parks. That's messed up.

All in all, the road became a lively nook in the city. I would sit in Axis and sip tea, a white mug with an impossibly beautiful tea bag floating in water the color of sunshine. I see the small buds of chamomile flowers through the veil of silken bag. Floating, flowers suspended in water, more art than drink. My mind drifts to a dream of the night before: marriage on Mars. In outerspace-ish silver get-ups with plastic bubble head coverings. I hate when my dreams dig into mid-century sci-fi set design for their style references. Awake, it makes me really doubt my imagination. I wonder about my subconscious mind—what is it up to? If the subconscious is free to ponder interstellar adventures, where's the robust creativity? The story of the dream is a wedding ceremony. I am a guest; my friend who is being wed is badly mauled—and I can see her leaking through her silver suit. It's the sort of dream that sticks with you. My colleague Colin, a no-nonsense industrial designer, sits down and asks what I am thinking about because I look so serious. Land art, I answer. I am thinking about land art.

Land art prompted that pitiful dream. I have been researching land art and *The Lightning Field* in New Mexico in particular and the San Francisco art critic Kenneth Baker came to my class to talk about his book on the topic, published by Yale University Press. *The Lightning Field* was designed by Walter De Maria and built with funds from the Dia Foundation. There is no way that sort of project would get funded today. It was built in 1977, and it is one kilometer by one mile in dimension. It is art in conversation with its political times, when the threat of thermo nuclear war was the Big Threat. The story and stakes of climate chaos are complex as a narrative and the politics of ecosystems shaped by peculiar needs to shirk connections. Reefs bleaching and dying? Antarctic food chains thrown out of whack? Trees in Djibouti filled with gauzy plastic bags, the land-based image for the oceans also filled with plastic bags leading to autopsies on pilot whales in Thailand where seventeen pounds of plastic are found in the poor bastard's stomach? Think of that whale: I'm not feeling so hot today, the pilot whale telegraphs to his squad. There are so many stories, so many images. In the end it does not matter if the listener can make causative connections or believes. It is like all development and ecosystem destruction: The facts are the facts are the facts—trees vanish, rains come, soils wash away, temperatures meander in an inebriated manner, storms gain a peculiar violence. And on and on.

EPISODE FIVE

*The deeper the blue, the more it summons man into infinity,
arousing his yearning for purity and ultimately transcendence.
Blue is the typical celestial color. Blue very profoundly develops the
element of calm.*—Vasily Kandinsky, On the Spiritual in Art

*It is a wholesome and necessary thing for us to turn again to the
earth and in the contemplation of her beauties to know of wonder
and humility.*—Rachel Carson

43 degrees F; wind from the SSW at 3 mph

May: On Drawing

A mile south of the Golden Gate Bridge the coastline
curves gently into land. Over the years, part of the
Presidio restoration has been the construction and
opening of trails that wind into the dunes and cliffs,
stairs and overlooks connecting the bridge to Baker Beach
and beyond in either direction. But when I first moved here
with my family the dune habitats were still obscured by many
more trees and non-native species of plants. Then, there were
still quail huddled under large jade bushes near where we
parked our car at night, offering their peculiar gurgling sound,
and there were still many days I could walk and see no one
in the woods or along roads. It was a different place. In our
neighborhood, on the western side of the park, the dominant
structure then was the abandoned Marine and Public Health
Service Hospital. It had become infamous through websites
trading in images of creepy abandoned buildings, artists and
amateurs making videos of its decrepit rooms, the tattered
curtains, medical equipment re-arranged to form psychotic
sculptures, squatters, walls of peeling paint and ripped
government signs then decorated with large graffiti, broken

glass formed a mosaic across once-polished floors. On the north face of the building, intact large window panes along the top floors were covered with graffiti and more elaborate screen prints. Anne Frank's hopeful face, her schoolgirl portrait from the book jacket, was in triplicate on the third floor, and she gazed at us as we drove down the hill each morning towards the children's schools. After drop-off, I would walk back down the hill and take photos of the building and then continue on to a café to write. I wondered how Anne came to be part of the fossil building, an art-project building. The photo brought to mind a visit to Amsterdam after I had been to sea with Greenpeace; a few of my shipmates were Dutch or lived in Holland between cruises. I went to the Anne Frank Museum there one day, and the museum had the letters from the US government refusing the Frank family entry to the US. They were form letters. The typed, personalized parts were not perfectly aligned, so the message there would be no path out to America had an agitated feel to it, as though the typist was working so quickly to refuse refugees, there was no time to properly line up the paper.

The hospital had started as a wood frame building in 1875, which was demolished and replaced by a 480-bed Georgian Revival building. In the early 1950s, two functional and aesthetic-crushing wings were built perpendicular to the main building, and the Georgian revival aesthetic was occluded. When demolition of the wings began—the Presidio renovating the building to become apartments—huge, clawed machines pounded the wings to dust, and the photo of Anne, and indeed all of the art, disappeared. My children and I would walk down after school and watch the machines pulverize the structure. The building held us in its thrall—horrible and sullen as a structure, the danger of wild humans living within a short walk of our home, the slowly fading photos of Anne. A giant conveyor belt and many empty metal dumpsters lined the hospital grounds and what the claw pulled down, a backhoe or bulldozer scooped into some sort of sci-fi metal and concrete shredder. Then mere chunks emerged, tattered structural remains, and fell into the dumpsters. *Amazing!* My son said, *We are so good at ripping things to bits.* We watched this rhythm of crude clawing, heaving conveyor belts, then the whole thing showered in a spray of water until the day it vanished and there was nothing where the two wings had so recently stood.

Then the Georgian Revival building revealed itself once again, like the good-looking sister forced to wear some unseemly gaudy costume, and stood regal and balanced. The original thinking, to design a hospital on this overlook with a clear view west, was clear. Lines of old trees occluding sun from native plants were removed, daylighting the creek bed towards Baker Beach, creating a sightline down a scraggly canyon, native plants that thrive on the sandy, cold dunes in the ocean wind and sun and fog. After this operation, we stand at the bottom of our street and look out at the neighborhood called the Richmond, an outer burg of the city, a mix of distinct ethnicities and nationalities, Vietnamese, Chinese, Russian, low buildings, streets festooned with overhead wires. In archival photos of the original hospital in 1875, the Richmond—which some histories say is named for Richmond, Australia—is surrounded by wind-swept dunes, dairy farms, race tracks, orphanages, and cemeteries. The hospital/apartment building is named The Landmark, and there is a concierge and a gas fire pit by the front door. There is no evidence of decay overlaid with drawings and scribbles and photo transfers, all now a whisper of memory. All the people who came together over hundreds of years to make that ruin, from the first people who planted the trees for the Army to the last people who squatted there with spray paint cans.

Robert Rathbun, my high school art teacher in Michigan, taught me the importance of materials for my work—a drawing itself an accumulation of choices, choices that start with, now I will draw. Now I will use a toothed sheet of pale green paper. Now I will use a piece of charcoal. He taught me how a colored sheet collaborated with my drawing and how the tooth of the paper affected not only the final drawing, but the experience of the artist's hand and then the experience of the viewer. He taught me about Dr. Ph. Martin's dyes and how I could radically change a painting of a cinnamon-bright tiger lily by using a Japanese watercolor brush with oils. In essence, he immersed me in the materiality of art and in conversation with concepts and surfaces.

On the floor of my office leans a large-format drawing that earned the young me a Gold Key in the statewide Hallmark competition and recalled how this win had pleased Rathbun. It is framed and matted, with both a grey and a pink matte. Several of our class won awards that year, including my good friend Dane who had taken the top prize in the state. Rathbun's art room was an incubator—it had large windows that overlooked the playing fields; the art department was on a higher floor in the back of the school, actual studios, and it was separated from the academic classes and had the feeling of climbing into a tower or aerie. Once I was a senior, I could take hours of art classes a day and so I did.

What Rathbun knew was boundless, and he taught me something about teaching that has never left my mind: Each student has a particular path or calling, and each needs her own muse or inner companions on the path. He assigned Kathe Kollwitz, an artist born in Prussia, as my research project. Kollwitz made a name for herself by taking on how women represent themselves, how the working class is represented, and did so through drawings, lithography, and self portraits. That she made this name for herself in times (she was born in the late nineteenth century and died in 1945) when women were meant to be captured in the gaze of men and not shining their own light on what they saw and reporting this out to the world was pointed out to me by Rathbun. I was too shy to ask why he had thought of her for me, and when I read about her, this question often pressed on my mind. Now, when I look at her work or read about her, I believe I can see what he was getting

at with the connection. She was a model of a fierce artist, a constant voice exploring and expounding on worker's rights and when I studied her work I felt how she believed in the power of drawing to do so. That me

Drawing of plants from Robert Rathbun's class at Grosse Pointe South High School; winner of Hallmark Gold Key Award

of high school was packed with political views and positions and outrage about social injustice. Rathbun would invoke her work much later, after my accident, imploring me to see other aspects of her work, how Kollwitz had experienced so much loss, had lost her son in World War I and how she spent much of her life to explore mourning through her art.

Rathbun pointed out how Kollwitz used mediums that made distribution of her work—towards advocacy—more fluid. She worked in woodblock prints and lithography, made illustrated posters around hunger, unemployment, laced with impassioned calls for help for those suffering most in post-war Vienna. At the point in my life that Rathbun introduced me to Kollwitz, I was more interested in the exacting form of drawing than what I saw as the more free form of painting. I liked how I could walk into my room at home and start to work immediately while oil painting took so much set up and so many supplies. And my sisters and mother would complain about the smell and mess. I liked the blacks and greys of the charcoal and the white chalk, the Conté crayon, combined on the textured paper. I liked the sounds of the pencil or charcoal on the page. Rathbun carefully showed me the intimate ways of the kneaded eraser, how it could be fashioned into a tiny point to remove material, revealing paper. And he was very strict about both application and removal of marks. How the marks, once made, could be faded by the kneaded eraser but always at the expense of the page.

We had a graphic design class, also taught by Rathbun, and we made album covers and political posters. I made a Coke bottle as Molotov cocktail, with the American flag as rag. Iran was about to fall and Óscar Romero had been murdered in El Salvador and everywhere there was talk about U.S. interference. How we interfered. Rathbun liked to talk about politics in the context of how I could make art around it all. How art would be a good way to ponder with nuanced depth the world I was seeing and feeling. We students had a loose and warm discourse with Rathbun. A girl named Jackie started calling him simply Buns, and soon others followed. I could never use that familiar term, and yet I saw him smile slightly when she called out across the room, *Buns,* come look at this.

Rathbun also had to contend with the general art-room class demeanor, more fringe players than in AP French—and requiring more discipline. I saw him become agitated only on a few occasions, usually with Dane, who talked feverishly and unceasingly and disturbed the generally focused, radio-music filled room with jokes and impressions. Sometimes we listened to Bach and other Baroque music, and sometimes we listened to the latest album by Yes or Queen. Dane would blather on, making up diddies, prompted by something he saw in the room, pulling stunts like grabbing a black magic marker and starting to draw and then singing, Got a black magic marker, to the tune of Santana's, "Black Magic Woman." There was the time he was on one of his reveries and he hit me on the head with a hammer and then spent an hour carefully drawing a hammer with a razor-point pen to give it to me as an apology. Among the other ten or so students, there was a boy named Brian, who came to class with messy long hair, filthy bare feet—a textbook hippy look which was intensely out of style in our swanky suburb. While we were usually amiable, Rathbun and Brian had a fight one day that was prompted by Rathbun's comments that all of Brian's art looked like derivatives of Yes album covers—and could he not come to class with a single original thought? And could he not come to class on time with shoes and stop walking around in those filthy feet in class—and it was the only day that I saw Rathbun completely lose it—red face, dramatically grabbing Brian, who had swung first at him with the intent to deck him, tossing Brian into the hall.

It was almost comic—Rathbun was tall and thin and in his pressed shirt, with an aquiline nose and a big shock of reddish-blond hair, he resembled a lithograph by Daumier or a character actor who would play either the reclusive concertmaster or the well-landed uncle in some British period piece. I knew he lived where we did, here in toney Grosse Pointe, in a carriage house belonging to a large mansion, and that he was not married. To the extent that we talked about it, it was understood that Rathbun was gay. The day he threw out Brian, then came back to the classroom and sat at his desk, red and agitated, I recall peering from behind my latest still life and watching him stack papers on his desk. Then he stood and said, "Brian does not take his art seriously enough. I am going to the principal's office to report his behavior." Everyone in the class looked up and looked down and started drawing or painting again.

It is time to walk. I walk, my thoughts wandering. Is each step a chance for memories to come to life, released from muscles, where we store them in calf, shin, lymph system jiggled into gear? I hear the waves pound on Baker Beach and sirens float across distant Geary Boulevard, and I think about how many people from Rathbun's art classes in Grosse Pointe went on to become artists and designers. He funneled people to New York, to The Cooper Union and Parsons and they came out the other side with something to say. I can find them on LinkedIn, and they are teaching art in colleges and making art and working in design agencies and being the people he hoped they would be. I trudge northeast and downhill, past the majestic home once reserved for the base commander—a stately brick home that rents for an obscene amount; the rent once quoted to me, somewhere around ten thousand dollars, by a rental agent in the Presidio. Because I had asked about it, she went into sales mode. She then added, but if you really want it, you can offer more than the asking rent to guarantee you get it.

The house has curtains—close to drapes but not entirely so. I recall Rathbun's particular interest in the draped fabrics of the still life, and how he would bring in velvets and brocades, and arrange them, and paint them for us to see the effect. He had an easy, painterly style, and would demonstrate how to sketch with oils—and then show us what happened to the sketch after days of careful painting, creating a brocade that you wanted to wrap around your shoulders. You see, he would say, there is a story in the material, always. Feel your materials and feel your story.

The brickwork of the Presidio is a bit of a peculiarity in San Francisco, a city of timber. In the mid-nineteenth century, wood from the Kauri tree was used to construct dwellings, both modest and elaborate. When the city burned in 1906, Kauri was used to rebuild it, shipped eastwards across the expanse of Pacific Ocean from its native home in New Zealand. They are tall, straight, magnificent trees, and their timber fueled the imagination of ship designers and waka builders. Kauri trees are the stuff of myth, literally. On a New Zealand government website: "Kauri features in a northern version of the creation story of Ranginui, the sky father, and Papatuanuku, the earth mother. At the beginning of time Rangi and Papa clung together, trapping their children in the darkness between them. The strongest child, Tane Mahuta (the god of the forest), pressed his shoulders against his mother and pushed upwards with his powerful legs, separating his parents and allowing light to enter and bring life to the world. Some northern Maori tribes say that his legs were the trunks of giant kauri trees."

The Army's deliberate use of brick and masonry over wood distinguishes the Presidio further from the city itself. Beyond the design of the forest, the design of the structures reminds me how the architecture falls on both ends of the spectrum—from the careful aesthetics of Fort Winfield Scott to the more perfunctory buildings that line the rest of the streets. I walk under the concrete span connecting the Golden Gate Bridge to Park Presidio Boulevard, past the stables, and thread through the Doyle Drive construction project (three cranes, the middle one about four stories tall lifting enormous black tubes.) Construction sites came onto my radar when my older son was about two, and one of our favorite activities was to stand and watch heavy machinery in action. Since that time, I try to stop and take in sites. They are a wonder of engineering design and a strange mash-up of high and low tech—men with red stop signs hand signal traffic along a single-lane road, amidst huge steel beams, rebar, concrete, and people with plans open across arms spread wide, engineers who will make sure this bridge on-ramp and tunnel can and will withstand millions of cars driving along as well as seismic shifts.

Parsing the walks and the opportunities of each day, how to be a more attentive mother, how to be more careful with my writing, how to do more of the things that matter like writing and reading books and knitting sweaters and walking. Why can't I earn a living wage for writing, I ask no one in particular in the woods. Why do market economies have such scant space for sustaining wide swathes of creative people without forcing them to endure the threat of economic annihilation year after year?

So I walk and allow my brain its saunter. And if I am in the right mindset, I can almost feel another walking at my side. I think Rathbun makes these walks with me some days, admiring the colors in his particular way. Look, he might say as the sun wanes, do you see how the leaves look almost like they are embroidered onto a lush deep pink velvet of sky? I also find myself reflecting on how Thoreau so beautifully wrote about walking. The stories and places of my life like to siphon into the walks, and perhaps this is part of what pushes me out into the forest each morning. The forest folds me into its cool arms and in a near-mystical way coaxes out memories, stories unspool. In high school, when I first read Thoreau, I recall despising his manner and the plodding way he recounted his life. I later found his name on a course reading list at the University of Michigan, and it was a course investigating American nature writing. The catalog suggested nature writing was a true American form, and the course would attempt to argue this. So I signed on. The teacher was a young woman whose name I do not recall, who loved Austin, Carson, Dillard, Emerson, Williams, Abbey, McPhee, Thoreau. I felt the heat of their voices. Then, when I delved into Thoreau's work again in graduate school at the University of Iowa, I read his writing more as a fellow traveler, a like-minded soul who saw the performance of it all, a revised, constructed voice, still-life construction writ large on the page. And then many years later, I was at a writing conference in Boston on a cold, snow-blown day, sitting nervously between the poets Camille Dungy and Liz Bradfield, on a panel of women who write about nature, waiting to read, listening to how and why wild places draw women to write about them.

I rented a car when the conference ended and drove alone across icy roads to Walden Pond, to walk the frozen pond's perimeter, to see the little house where Thoreau wrote. His ideas would fade from the canon of American literature, then surface in the twentieth century, when the climate is changing and the culture is slipping at a terrifying pace into a structure called the Web. Thoreau rebuked the railway, perhaps a visible expression of the Web, a system of conduits that sped up the world and changed how we understood not only time but what it meant to be human. The small cabin where he performed his hermit's life is there—Mrs. Emerson did his wash, and others brought him food and news of the world—and then his return to formal society where he revised and revised and revised.

There is a gift shop at Walden Pond, and I have to admit I fetishize gift shops at museums and historic sites. We monetize the stories of civil society, art, past lives, experiences in the gift shops of the world. On this cold, grey day, it is only me, the volunteer shopkeeper (his tag explained), and a tall, bearded German man who has come to Walden Pond on a pilgrimage. The German man has a lot of questions about Thoreau, and he is not able to grasp that the shopkeeper is not an expert on Thoreau. *I am an enthusiast,* the shopkeeper says to the German man, *and not able to answer your questions.*

The questions are specific and intense. As a research scholar myself, I do not know if anyone could answer these questions definitively. I buy some postcards and a key chain and retreat to the parking lot. Outside in the cold, damp air, looking at the snowy, ice-covered pond now flanked by a railroad track, I think about how hard Thoreau's life was. How his brother died of lock jaw and how Thoreau stayed by his side during this slow and painful demise. How he never married and some scholars say he died a virgin. How he quit teaching because he refused to engage in the regular beatings of pupils that the vicars demanded. How when he was at Harvard it was a raucous, loud, fist-fight driven ecosystem of ideas and rhetorical posturing and taking a stand and holding it was the way of the world for a young scholar.

"I WISH TO SPEAK a word for nature, for absolute Freedom and Wildness, as contrasted with a freedom and Culture merely civil—to regard man as an inhabitant, or a part and parcel of Nature, rather than a member of society. I wish to make an extreme statement, if so I may make a emphatic one, for there are enough champions of civilization; the minister, and the school-committee, and every one of you will take care of that."

The author at Walden Pond during the Association of Writers & Writing Programs conference in nearby Boston

Thoreau, in the essay "Walking," speaks about how the word saunter was first a specific label for people walking towards the

Holy Land, on a pilgrimage towards God. He also liked to call people out, Saint Francis style, for behaving in idiotic ways, for participating in shallow pursuits, for giving up: living lives of quiet desperation. Which is what makes his voice so engaged and at times, disturbing. He is calling out people and I feel if he were in the room, he would be calling out me. Are you a Walker or are you an Idler? Worse yet, are you a Vagabond?

They who never go to the holy land in their walks, as they pretend, are indeed mere idlers and vagabonds, but they who do go there are saunterers in the good sense, such as I mean.

Here is where I remember. I remember the art teacher who had so much heart we were allowed to make terrific messes. I recall the day I came to the studio and saw that Rathbun had taken my recent painting, a still life of a copper kettle, strawberries and brown butter crock, and elevated it to the highest in-class honor: The easel above his desk. And in that moment, I saw what he meant when he said, how if we try, we could find and articulate a particular beauty in the ordinary.

I remember running into Rathbun the summer after senior year. A group of us were at a lakeside park in Grosse Pointe, it was close to the time the park closed, and we were furtively drinking beer and smoking. He came along the path, wearing short cutoff jeans and a pink polo shirt. He was tan, and his legs looked gangly and long. He was accompanied by a blond man also in cut-off shorts and polo shirt and very white leather tennis shoes. Rathbun stopped for a minute, although he did not have to. He wanted to know how we were enjoying summer. And then he gently admonished us for our behavior and strolled off into the dark, sauntered even, towards the sailboats, the lake, with a fringe of Canada visible in the gloaming beyond.

NOTEBOOK FIVE

I walk and a big wind is building and the temperature has dropped about seven degrees in the last hour. Monterey Pine branches litter the trail, knocked clear off by a blistering storm the night before, gangs of cones clinging together. Long strides, moving quickly but with care. I have my Detroit Tigers hat on to keep my hair from whipping into my mouth, an unpleasant reality of life with hair in these woods. I am nuts mad for baseball and my team is the Detroit Tigers and my adopted team is the San Francisco Giants; I have hats for each. The word, Detroit,—from French, d'etroit, meaning "the straits" as in the strait connecting Lake St. Clair with Lake Erie—means relocation and dislocation and home all at once. We relocated to the Mitten State when I was sixteen. It was here that I completed high school at Grosse Pointe South and met Robert Rathbun and convalesced from my horrible car accident in Florida and then attended art school at Wayne State University as a commuter and then transferred to the University of Michigan. That all happened in a few short years.

It was here, I presume, that I first began considering the emotional life of a landscape, or rather, the emotional life of a certain woods in Maryland I had stared at and walked in for most of my childhood. My father lost his job, and then we moved to Michigan so he could be an editor for *The Detroit News*. Ripped out of my woods, driven across Pennsylvania and blizzard-fogged Ohio—I recall the terror and wonder of observing heaving windshield wipers trying to move snow and sleet off the windshield as my father steered our Ford station wagon along the Ohio State Turnpike with big rigs jackknifed on either side—the feeling was one that the world had become a complete and utter fiction. How could my landscape, my whole forest simply disappear? In Grosse Pointe I learned how loneliness goes: How to listen to the Tigers on the radio on a Saturday night because I had no friends, how to swim in a cold lake alone, how to feel the feeling that new places erase the self. Were memories so ethereal, so pegged to what we see, smell, if we change what we see and smell, do we effectively erase a part of who we are?

One of the ubiquitous Presidio tree species, the Monterey Pine, *pinus radiata*, tells its story of survival through a fossil-cone record. Asymmetrical cones covered with large bulbous umbos—knobs protruding—smooth to the touch. Once buried they release hydrogen and oxygen atoms as water, carbon dioxide, and methane gas. How the past is the key to how we understand the present.

When healthy, the Monterey pine can be four feet wide at the base and reach up a hundred or more feet into the air. It also emits a particular sound: On hot days I can hear a distinctive cracking sound as a handful of its cones open. The taxonomic category known as California closed-cone pines, to which the Monterey belongs, have many cones that remain sealed with resin, stay closed for decades. They may sit unopened for years, then open and remain on the tree. Botanists have a name for this, serotiny, and the thinking is that this is an adaptation to dry climates with periodic fires. Then forest fires come raging through tree canopies, and the tree's resin seal melts. When the fire abates, the cones quickly release a year-old supply of seeds. While the mature tree dies in the fire, new trees grow from these seeds, speedily repopulating the area, moving more swiftly than neighbor species.

I stop and pick up a large Monterey pine cone. The story of this pine, like all stories, those of tree or person, change as more information is unearthed. More recent climate records gathered from the Atlantic, Arctic, and Pacific cover hundreds of thousands of years, and include gases trapped in the ice, datable to individual years. They tell a tale of eleven ice ages over the last million years. While stands of wild Monterey pines remain in only a handful of locations, under threat from climate, goats, and a deadly fungal disease, domesticated Monterey pines in the U.S. find homes in backyards and smaller ones live briefly as Christmas trees. It is also a tree that makes a lot of money for people all over the world as the most-planted conifer. These are genetically manipulated trees, to create straight, fast-growing individuals to be cut down and cut up and sold. I guess the Presidio forest falls somewhere in between the true wild and the tree-industrial complex.

Rathbun told me once that the one thing sculptors never make is a tree: Too complex, those branch systems. Human form more approachable for symmetry and balance or its skewing.

As I walk with the Monterey pines of the Presidio, on a May day, it is the Star Wars Day, May the Fourth be with you. But my mind is restless; a May from memory is near at hand. A May when my singular goal is to get home in time to go to prom. I am in St. John's Hospital in Detroit, nearby to our home, after a car accident over senior year spring break in Florida. The crash happened on a state road somewhere near the city of Lake Wales, in central Florida. We were driving to Grosse Pointe after a week at the beach. My best friend, Meg, was in the car, and she died. I was the driver. Our friend Carole was in the backseat, and she walked away unscathed. I think back on the me of that May as I walk in the woods of the Presidio. I have a black notebook with me; Walt Whitman's lines are in this notebook, from his less-read, later work, *Sands at Seventy, The Lost Pilot, Steaming* in the northern rapids, an old St. Lawrence reminiscence.

A sudden memory-flash comes back, I know not why.

Next to Whitman, I have written a line from the Scottish naturalist James Hutton: The present is the key to the past. In the late eighteenth century Hutton argued that erosion and other modern processes could leave behind records in rocks.

The thing about scars is that they are ugly. Making sense of their ugliness can offer a lifetime of work. I have never counted the scars on my body, but I know each one as a story. The vertical scar on my abdomen that hooks an inch sideways at the top was where they removed my spleen and part of my liver in emergency surgery after the car crash. There are two drain scars adjacent to this line. The scar on my left hip is where they removed part of the hip bone to graft it onto my neck. The scar across the front of my neck is where they cut through, Frankenstein style, to apply a notched piece of hip bone to my cervical spine. The joint of my left arm bears a scar where they inserted the cut-down IV, after the hand-top IV leaked into my flesh. That leakage was very painful.

I walked and pondered this, sat down on a felled tree and wrote some notes, as another Detroit memory streamed into view: How on a torpid June day, about a week before rains would stream down over the Midwest and cause great floods, urging rivers to take over tree, building, land, I stood in Detroit Metro Airport with my son Will waiting for a connecting flight to home to San Francisco and the Presidio. That day in Detroit the outline of the tree line looked familiar—and yet, could it be? I had not been in that airport in years. As I looked at the bright green leaves seemingly pasted against a puce sky, I thought of another time in this same airport, in another early summer, in what felt like another lifetime and I pressed my finger tips, splayed against the glass as if to remind myself that I was here now.

I recall being wheeled towards St. John's hospital doors—it was the first time I had been under the Michigan sky since the crash. At the door to the hospital, Dr. Jewel with a beaming smile stood awaiting my arrival; a family friend, stout and grey-bearded, Jewel was a neo-natal surgeon. His area of expertise was delivering babies the size of his hand. Jewel recommended the pediatric ward and not orthopedics because the pediatric ward would be more upbeat and cheery for a young patient looking at a long stay. They settled me in a two-bed room by the window. Sheri was my three-year-old roommate. She had kidney cancer, her parents explained, and was used to sharing a hospital room. She was back for yet another round of surgery. Bald from treatments, she raced around, chattering and whipping some sort of stuffed toy over her head. Because I was flat on my bed, staring at the ceiling, I saw bits of her in my peripheral vision, pale skin, the air moved as she ricocheted around my bed while her mother told her not run. She came and stood at my side and I turned my aching neck a bit and saw her tired, waxy face, the dark circles around her eyes, and in them a look of fear. Of me. I smiled and said *Hi*, tried but could not raise an arm. She ran away. Over the next weeks we would become companions, visiting like this when all of the others were gone. She would climb out of her bed and come stand by my bed and stare at me. Sometimes she would put her stuffed animal on my arm. Sometimes she would hold my hand.

Her father and I watched the Tigers play on the wall-mounted television when Sheri was in treatment. He explained how you could live with a small amount of kidney, and they had removed all the cancerous kidney and then there were transplants. He would say this and then go back to watching the game. But then it was in my mind.

There were a lot of comments around the length of my stay, most of which were answered by, "We'll see." No one talked about the fact that there were three people in the car and one was dead. No one talked about how I had been the car's driver and how there were no other cars involved and the only reason they could find for the car to flip out of control was a blow-out of a rear tire causing me to veer off the road then flip out of control. I do not know why we crashed. The state trooper who investigated it said to me: It was an accident.

This was May, and my goal was to get home in time to go to prom. Does this sound insane? Yes, this sounds insane; however it completely defines in a few words my mindset. I was going to get home and go to prom with someone good. I had already made a mental list of my possible dates. First on the list was Peter. I loved that guy. The fact that he liked me, but didn't love me, and he attended dances and parties with me as a fall-back position, he favored the bleached-blond twins notorious in our class for putting out. There was the cute wrestler named Rich and the basketball player named Johnny. I wish I could say that I was thinking profound thoughts about what was happening to my body, but the fact is: No. I was praying a lot, and the outcome of the prayers was hopefully prom and college. No threat I was going to become an inspirational speaker.

Rathbun stood at the foot of my Stryker frame in St. John's Hospital and said: Tell me what you have learned as an artist from this? Many years later as I reflect on that moment, Rathbun standing, looking at me intently—was he trying not to cry—from the foot of the metal frame where my young body was being stretched to allow for spinal cord healing—a rig that flipped me like a pancake so that bedsores would not form. I recall at the time thinking it was an idiotic question and that maybe the answer was that I was not an artist anymore. That the accident had taken that from me. But instead I said, I think I see the color blue in a different way. And I indicated with a finger on my right hand the window on to my right. I could not use my hand to gesture; my arms were partially paralyzed.

He looked out the window, looked out very solemnly. Very solemn and formal. Aquiline nose, pressed shirt, hands clasped in front of him. He was the only teacher who came to see me in the hospital, and he came to see me more than once. He said. Ah, yes, it has enhanced your color sense.

What I appreciated about his visits, in the hospital and at home, was his formality. His visits were intended as an educational moment, to help me see that this was not simply an accident, but a time to learn. It was a very hopeful countenance, one that said without saying it: You will heal and you will be back in the world and you will be making art again.

Many months later, when I was better enough to get out into the world, one of the first things I did was take a night-time painting class at The War Memorial in Grosse Pointe. I had my oils and my brushes, and I was rusty. But the subject was tiger lilies, an inspiring choice for me, so I broke out the Japanese water-color brushes that Rathbun had taught me to use with oils and began to sketch with paint. Then I backfilled with a deep gorgeous midnight blue so the orange flowers sprang from the canvas. The art teacher did not find this sketch as successful as I did. She wanted me to control the work. *Show more mastery,* she urged.

The next time Rathbun came to visit me, I showed him the painting. *She's right,* he added, when I told him about the critique. *But I hope you told her you have a mastery of the still life and now you are moving on to your own specific story of color.* Then he nodded at me. It's the sad part of being a self-focused college student; I would stop by my high school to say hello to him when I was home for a weekend, but I never suggested we have coffee or a meal or get the class together over winter break. Years later, I tried to track down his address. It was then I learned from the high school that Rathbun had died of AIDS, but I was told there was a scholarship fund at the high school set up in his name. It helped many students attend art school.

One thing I never speak about is how I was afraid of dying alone in the dark. I could not tell people about this fear. So I told God. An elderly nun had pinned a Saint Jude medal on my hospital gown, Saint Jude the saint for the hopeless who need hope. My mother would unpin it and take it away, and then the nun would come back and pin on another the next day. Some sort of icon-battle.

I did not tell the nurses that nighttime was, in my opinion, the worst time to die. No one who works in the hospital needed to hear this, the Irrational Cheerleader reminded me. They all had enough to worry about! There were people in here dying, like Sheri! I was getting better. What did I have to complain about? So I kept my silent vigil, trying to stay awake 'til dawn. Many days I succeeded, watching late-night television, faking sleep when the nurse came in. I loved the night nurse in particular; she was soft and round. She would sit with me and talk. We would talk for what seemed like hours. She had a family, a husband and two young children, and she liked working nights because this way she arrived home when they were getting up for school, made them a hot breakfast, and got them off to school then she would go for a bike ride around her neighborhood, and then she would come home and go to bed. She slept all day then would get up when the children came home from school. Then she would get ready to come to the hospital after reading to them and putting them to bed. She would sit with me and watch late-night talk shows, and then she would turn off the TV and leave my light on low and say, Just close your eyes. It's good to rest. I will check on you every 15 minutes so get some shut-eye. When she stood up, she always adjusted her white polyester pants, snapping the elastic waistband. Sound and memory are immutably linked. Snapping elastic is the sound of love.

EPISODE SIX

This is the forest primeval.—Longfellow, "Evangeline"

You begin to realize that the important determinant of any culture is after all the spirit of the place.—Lawrence Durrell

June: On Place

In the Presidio Archive, a former cavalry stable built of brick in 1914, on the road leading down through the trees towards Crissy Field, across from the famed Presidio Pet Cemetery, a turquoise sign hangs from the ceiling: Explore the wilderness . . .

Files stacked around me hold an extraordinary range of Army records, menus, supply orders, days and times of Army exercises, where the guns are, where they want to put the guns, how cold the Fort Point quarters are, granular and banal stories of life in the Presidio dating to the days of Spanish occupation. What was this ecology before the trees? In 1847, stories of struggles to create a habitable commune and generalized views of what this meant to the report's author; brief summaries of this bit of Alta California sounding like a scene from an Ingmar Bergman film, "acres of grasses and wildflowers; horses and cattle grazed on treeless hills and dales. Sand shifted." The reports describe lacquered cannonballs lining roads and paths; officers' wives, assisted by post gardeners, planting bright flower gardens and shrubs around homes. None of this helped the stank or the wind. In one of the accounts from 1859 an unnamed officer writes to a colleague that the Presidio has been denuded of scrub oaks and other arboreal life by earlier residents in need of fuel. They had left no trees for ornamental use. It brought to mind my beloved Maryland.

Twenty-four years after this anonymous account, Major William Albert Jones surveyed the same land and wrote a plan. Jones' forest plan was a design response to the stories in the folders, hundreds of accounts of "omnipresent sand." How Pacific winds blew sand—a wind said to drive soldiers mad. Details of odiferous swampy lands, and cold, dank winds.

I study a replica of the original drawing.

Picture this, because this is what was there when the drawing was imagined: On the Bay side, there is The Swamp, 110 acres along the bay. Flooded by tides, filling with large shallow lakes when the rainy season descends, with a twelve-foot-high sand ridge that ran along the Bay side. The waters of the Bay routinely breached the sand wall, creating standing water. Good luck finding any shelter—the dunes covered with low-lying scrub, dotted with cattle and horses, grazing. Illness was connected in part to bad smells, and bad smells came from standing water. (They were partially right. Foul, standing water was often a breeding ground for disease-carrying mosquitoes and other pests. What took time to understand was that it wasn't the smell making them sick, but insect-borne disease.)

Imagine a rough desk, poorly lit by a single flame flickering in the wind. A cast-iron pot belly stove with a small fire warming the room, chasing the damp. Some horrible stew of sinewy beef seasoned with salt and some mealy potatoes with watery coffee to wash it down. He wears a neatly pressed uniform, wool slightly scratchy against the skin. See Major Jones: A man on a mission and hear the sound of his pen scratching across the page—laying out the plan. Pen pushes forward. At night, the ideas come to him, so many phantoms. He leans over the desk. Not only will the forest add to the beautification of the Presidio, it will perform the magnificence of government. His predecessors in beautification had planted barley and lupine on the dunes. Jones swipes his pen and draws the curvilinear forms of dune, rising. As he draws, he feels their lift and movement with his toes. Next, the creeks are drawn, heavy black lines traced east towards the watershed.

Then the real artistry comes into place: How it is to be planted. Jones closes his eyes. Takes a breath. Maybe smokes a little tobacco. He can see it all, as if from thousands of feet above. The magnificence of the headlands, moving across the strait named Golden Gate by John Charles Frémont, sparkling seas: Then. Then a great curtain of dark green, so many trees to curtain the winds and create a majestic theater of civic power and control. Even in those days there was free flow of San Franciscans into the park, a bit of nature to escape the "Barbary Coast" that was the city. Jones wanted the place to be welcoming to civilians, too.

Jones marked large trees as a circle bisected by a line. The head of a screw.

Three large dots form a triangle: large bush
Clusters of three small dots: small bush
Trees and bushes circled to create autonomous areas
Numbered and lettered

At the Arguello Gate, flowering peach trees first, then in front of them, hydrangeas and lilacs. After the flowers, "fill in the space on the righthand side so as to make the first part of the drive entering the reservation dark and somber."

A theater of nature. It is visible today, as you enter the Arguello Gate into the Presidio, past the golf course and dark woods open to a grand, blue San Francisco Bay.

When he completes his plan, Jones sends it to members of Congress and San Francisco civic leaders to garner support. He receives word from U.S. Representative John Coburn, chairman of the House Military Committee, that the Presidio "must give you an opportunity to produce the most charming effects, which will prove to be a blessing to San Francisco and her visitors for hundreds of years after you are gone."

I bring paper and a box of colored pencils to the archive and I trace the plan and then fill it in with viridian and cadmium. I alternate between reading letters and coloring and in this state of concentration, gaze at the plan that I now walk in.

On California's first Arbor Day late in 1886, school-children planted about 3,000 tree slips donated by mining magnate Adolph Sutro. It is the largest mass planting to date in the Presidio. The first Artillery Regimental Band welcomed 4,000 women and children; the Army had dug 5,000 holes for the trees.

The Presidio was the Army's first large-scale tree planting and landscaping effort. Ten years after it began, the Army was looking for 60,000 more trees to plant. In 1892, William Montrose Graham was post commander and complained the trees were interfering with military operations, "Another evil arising from the extensive tree planting and which is only beginning to be felt, as the earlier plantings are attaining considerable size, is the dense thickets that are being formed, which makes shelters and secure hiding places for the tramps that infest the reservation." By 1901, Maj. Gen. S.B.M. Young, commanding general of the Department of California, wanted a larger, professional plan for the Presidio. He had consulted Gifford Pinchot, the storied leader of what was to become the U.S. Forest Service, and asked for a specialist to help. By then, the Army had planted 100,000 trees in the Presidio.

Jones's plan is still visible in the twenty-first century; his version of nature stuck. Who was he? A West Point graduate, an engineer, originally from Missouri. The Presidio forest and a mission he lead from Utah northward to Yellowstone in 1873, discovering the Togwotee Pass in the Wind River Range, a new, southerly passage to the Yellowstone Basin, are considered his notable Army accomplishments. There is no big statue of Jones outside the archives like there is of Yoda outside nearby Lucas Arts. The designer of our days in the Presidio oddly receded yet omnipresent like sand, serpentinite, wind.

Walking up the hill to our home, the hills tangles of wild blackberries and poison oak. People come to harvest the blackberries, and there are several people astride bikes plucking and eating berries. I walk through my favorite stand of trees, one that has become terribly enfeebled by the lack of thinning and the poor soil quality. The light is cold and indifferent across the too-thin trunks, these slowly starved trees, and yet the palette created, moss, viridian, alizarin, generates another sort of energy. It is among the most photographed groves because of this light and on this walk there is a young bride posing in a yellowed vintage satin gown, hands folded, holding calla lilies, head bowed in this silent woods, and it is beautiful.

NOTEBOOK SIX

The memory plays like a film, one where a camera, clearly mounted on a low-flying drone, moves slowly in over an undeveloped landscape near Lake Wales, central Florida. I was there in the original version, the one called real, as opposed to remembered, but because of circumstances soon to be revealed, I may not have the best recollection of the actual facts. I am somehow alive yet also half under a dark green Ford Capri. A lone house stands not far from the state highway. It is run down, and old auto parts are in the front yard. The house is weathered and grey. The man who lives there, whose name no one seems to recall, sells bait. I know there must be lakes and rivers nearby, where people use the bait, but in this shot, we see none of that. This part I have verified: The bait-shack man is talking on the phone with his mother, looking out the large window from his kitchen table. (Was he smoking, drinking coffee? Was the kitchen decorated in 1970s harvest gold? Was the phone gold with a long, stretched-out cord? Can the man sit at the kitchen table and talk or walk to the electric range and make some Hamburger Helper, or even walk into the living room and sit on the plaid sofa and watch television shows?) He calls his mother early each Saturday to see if she is OK or if she needs anything. She doesn't live all that far away.

Then he sees a lone car tumble off the highway, surging up and like a whale he saw recently on *Mutual of Omaha's Wild Kingdom*. Whales fly like that because they are in love or simply playing, the man recalled the narrator stating. Mom, I have to go, he said. There's been a bad accident down on the road. Call the fire department and have them send an ambulance. The man doesn't think twice, he leaves the room, opens the metal storm door to the car port and begins jogging down the hill. Maybe I should've brought a blanket, or some water, an ax he thinks. I don't have any tools with me. But he is closing in on the scene and it looks bad and he stops thinking in the abstract about what he needs. The day is hot, humid, almost like summer although it is still late spring. Smoke rises from the upside down car. A head of long brown hair emerges from the back seat window, inches out the front window like a caterpillar; she is wrapped in a quilt. She clutches the quilt around her as though it is winter and holds a large plastic bag of bubble gum. She looks like she has been asleep. She stares at him and does not speak. The other one, the one he cannot take his eyes off of, is sort of half under, half out from under the car. She has short blond hair and her eyes are open and she is trying to talk.

When he leans down next to her, she says, *Heavy,* or she seems to say heavy her voice is in a strange way. Almost a gurgle. Or maybe it's *Help me.* The man could not be sure. Out of the corner of his eye he sees a third one, and this one looks real bad. No way is that one alive. He thinks it's a girl, too, but cannot be too sure. The scene cuts. We cut from looking up into the face of the old bait man trying to hear the girl under the car, to a 14-year-old boy on the red Schwinn bike. The bike has a glittery banana seat and white rubber hand grips, both of which are covered with the grey veins of age. The bike is a hand-me-down but still takes the boy where he wants to go. The car passed him as he pumped along the shoulder and after it whizzed by he bumped back onto the road. There's never anyone on the road at this time of day, never really anyone on this road ever. He cranks the pedals. His friend Derek just got an above-ground pool, and he is going to help fill it with the hose. Then they will swim in the ice-cold water and eat ice cream sandwiches. Derek's mother always makes them eat some of what she calls real food, too, the same sandwich, white bread with a little mayonnaise and two slices of orange cheese, cut through in a diagonal. Then they get a handful of Fritos and a Dixie cup of Kool-Aid. The boy hears the sound of the crash before he sees the smoke. Then he sees and smells the smoke. There's a lot of smoke and when he comes around the bend the first thing he thinks is, that car is going to blow sky high.

The old man is thinking the same thing. He looks over at the brown-haired girl and says, *Hey, do you think we should move her before the ambulance gets here?* And when she doesn't answer, he says, *Did you have a lot of gas in your tank?* This question the girl hears and she says, *Yes, we just stopped and filled up and got coffee and donuts and bubble gum.*

Damn, the man says to himself. He wished he could understand her. But can he move the blond girl alone? As he begins looking around for something, something he can use to level up the car a little with one hand and drag her with the other, he hears a young voice say, *Whoa!*

The man turns towards the sun and sees the boy, astride his bike. He says, *Well, son, I need your help moving this girl from under the car. All you need to do is grab under her shoulders and move her out when I rock the car back. Got that?*

The boy drops his bike. The man expected the boy to resist, to claim some sort of unwillingness, but then he remembered in times like these, people just act on commands.

The blond girl was trying to talk again. Trying to make a whisper and each time it sounded like the car was taking more of breath. Time to move her.

The man said, *On three!* And then he used his legs and back to lift the car, creating a small wedge of room and as he did so, he heard the wail of the ambulance and said to himself, thank God almighty. And then the boy was pulling and dragging the blond girl, who turned out to be very small, less than 100 pounds he figured, out from under the car. The girl could not seem to move any part of herself. He guessed some of those bones must have been crushed. He didn't know what to say to her, although she stared at him, as though waiting for him to tell her something important. The man hugged the boy. *You did it,* he said. *You and me did it!*

The ambulance men ran over to the blond girl. They started talking to her, but she stared back at them, blinking and not even trying to talk.

They started to talk quickly into their radios and had a board and loaded her onto it. They were talking to the girl in the quilt who had walked a ways down the road alone, and then they were also aware of the dead girl in front of the accident and they covered her with a blue sheet. And then the board went onto the ambulance, and one of them hopped in back and one of them slammed doors and then they were away. The state trooper was coming by and get some sort of report, they added, so you two just stay close. Then they backed up and helped the brown-haired girl into the ambulance. And away they sped, lights and screeching sirens. Then the trooper arrived and he was moving more slowly, talking into his radio, putting on his hat, looking out on the road behind him and then making little marks on the road.

Across town, Dr. Ancaya kissed his wife good bye and threw his golf clubs into the trunk of his sedan. As he started off for the country club, he heard the crisp, electric call of the siren. Ambulance sirens mean something different to ER doctors in small towns. He was the doctor on call at the Lake Wales Hospital ER. He would get paged. But if he left for the ER now, Dr. Ancaya would meet the ambulance there as it arrived.

Now the film of memory, begun with the wide view of the landscape, and one where the sun or camera angle obscured faces, takes on a different view. We never saw the boy's face. We never really saw the old man's face. No one recalls their names. If the family had any of these reports or records, they were destroyed long ago and the details forgotten. We can only imagine what was in their hearts. They appeared, as angels or other saviors do at that make- or break-it moment. (Later we will learn that without their having the courage to move her small body, many feel certain she would have died. The car was close to squeezing out her last breath.) The ambulance man, the one who rides in the back is more clear; he has soft, curly, light-brown hair. His name is Chris. At the hospital, there is a Mexican orderly in the ER. (Comes to her room each day to see her once she is out of the coma, and so they become friends, and it is within these conversations she comes to know his family is back in Mexico and that he wants to be a doctor one day.) His name is Martin, which he pronounces Mar-teen.

It is his job to get her to sign the release papers that allow them to do the surgeries she now needs to save her life. Until this point, she did not have a sense there was any real problem. Sure the car flipping, the getting flung out the window and the car landing on her really felt peculiar, but now it felt much easier to breath. Her head aches and her mouth is super dry and the world reminds her of how things look after she jumped off the high dive for the first time in Maryland and opened her eyes in the twelve-foot deep water. Bubbles. Movement. Pushing hard to the surface for air. Martin holds the form. She tries to raise her right hand and then the panic sets in, a sharp if muddy sense things are all wrong.

I cannot move my arms, she says to Martin in the gurgly voice. His face shows that Martin thinks things are pretty bad, too. He holds her hand ,and she sees a weird black x emerge on the white page and the shape of this letter, sort of a v, sort of x, an indeterminate nonletter, a symbol or glyph, word from on high that whatever she thought was going on, whatever things seemed to be, well, things are far worse. There is no imagination to cover this experience. So she starts to pray.

Martin then begins to cut off her clothes with scissors, he starts at the neckline and begins to cut down towards the waist. What is she wearing? A red T-shirt that says The Song Remains the Same. It is the class-trip shirt she designed and had silk-screened for twenty of their classmates. She is tan and thin and eighteen and has just been in Fort Lauderdale, Florida for ten days for spring break. Through the haze, thoughts about how she doesn't want Martin to see her body naked, a body she has never considered very "good"—lacking in attention-getting features like large breasts. She feels suddenly shy, forgetful of everything else going on. This window of shyness she later recalls as funny. To be so self-conscious when she was bleeding to death internally. As he cuts off her shirt, she sees there is huge bruise across her abdomen, a map of a dark purple and red sea.

Then they are all around, looking down, Dr. Ancaya, blond nurses who smell like lemons. She is given drugs and falls asleep. She sleeps while they work in that Florida hospital to find where all the blood is coming from and to stop it. She will not wake for many days, and when she does the world will taste and smell and sound the same. But its look and feel will be entirely different. The entire earth and sky will have shifted.

This is an essay I wrote about the accident, which was published when I was in graduate school at the University of Iowa. I was going to write a memoir of the accident. Of course over the years I realized that this was all I had to say about the story of accident, that the accident was a proper noun, it had a look and a feel and an effect and a personality. I thought about how we name storms that destroy people's lives and the known world of nature and how we don't have language for other sorts of things that happen to our bodies. How the technology of language is so limited when it comes to the complexities of the human heart and mind and how we use these blunt-force words like death and loss and accident. Perhaps this is why Monterey pine's cone, designed to be super-heated melting resin, dispenses seeds after the fire, to make a new stand of pines even as the mother tree dies. Perhaps this is why when I walk I feel so at home in this forest and why the forest does not appeal to me as metaphor or retreat but as fact and essence of faith that life is to be well lived.

How Air Moves

I watch the back of my mother's head in the mirror, how she turns slightly to one side to check if my skirt's white bow is even and centered. The skirt is soft over my rigid fake form. Underneath, a body cast—a molded tank top extending down over my hips, my new exoskeleton, my nautilus, crawled into, where I live now. A big bright yellow sun cracks through the bedroom window where my mother dresses me. Today I am going to the senior prom. Today I managed to walk up three steps by myself.

Here is what I know: I have been home for sixteen days after forty-six in the hospital. The hospital that emerges before my eyes as I slowly recall, ah yes, the car I traveled in rolled and rolled and rolled.

Jacob, a seventy-three-year-old man living fifteen miles north along this Michigan lakeshore, begins writing me letters each day. I now have close to twenty-four of them, all on pale blue paper with a scrolling embossed border and curving penmanship laid down with a fountain pen. He writes because my story appeared in a newspaper column along with my address: Tell her you are thinking about her. You know the sort—the local paper's columnist taking someone under his wing. Now I have many correspondents but none as devoted as Jacob. He gives me ideas about things to think about, tells me how the day's weather is shaping up. Try recording the weather every day, he tells me, it is a fun hobby. I now know there are forces at work on the very air we breath, moving it around, slamming it up and down the length of the planet. This force has a name and, I imagine, a face as well.

While the weather does its thing, all these high and low pressures, the endless iterations of cloud, my broken neck figures out how to heal. My mother pushes milk, because milk builds strong bones. So I eat a lot of vichyssoise and cream of potato, canned soup made with milk, comforting white foods eaten from bowls, spooned into my mouth by my older sister Beth while I am propped in a bright green and orange slipcovered chair in the den. Beth watches the evening news, summer stories about pleasure boats caught halfway to Canada, nearly run down in the shipping lane by Ford freighters. She scoops white liquid, doesn't notice the soup running down my chin, mops in broad strokes across my face. *Hey listen,* I try to tell her, *we're not waxing the car here.*

But I need the help. I cannot lift the heavy milk container from the fridge; I cannot even lift the straw that goes into my glass. Laurie the Cheerful works on this each morning in the physical therapy suite conveniently located in the hospital's basement. She calls me her star patient. *Boy,* she says, playing with the zipper on her uniform, pulling it up an inch to the collar, then down a half inch, back and forth talking, *We'll sure fool those doctors!*

When I was an inpatient, they would line up in our wheelchairs to wait for physical therapy. It was mainly old women and me, women with thin strands of white and grey hair combed haphazardly over naked scalps, with purple veins looking like yarn under their skin, knitting up and around bones now a yellow sawdust composite, ready to give way. One brings a naked Baby Tender Love doll with her every morning. The orderly's name is Kirk, and he lines up our wheelchairs. Kirk is a thin guy around twenty with feathered-back, parted-in-the-middle hair, sporting a pale-blue smock worn over white pants and a T-shirt. Kirk always stops and talks to Baby Tender Love. For some reason his talking to that doll makes me want to bawl. Maybe I remembered my own Baby Tender Love. All I know is, each day I listen to him, in a genuinely nice voice, say, *How is your baby today?* He crouches down by the naked doll and says, *Hey, how's your baby today?*

Once inside, the other people, moving, capture my imagination. New elbows or knees, working them out as though they are the bionic man. Boy, will they fool the doctors, I think. One treadmilling man looks like Tom Selleck. I see that while I can stare at him, he cannot stare at me, or even look my way. Right now, I am fooling no one. I weigh about 80 pounds, have a neck broken in three places, and may never use my arms again. Here is what I know: Right now I am not fooling anyone. In therapy, my arms are raised over my head. I never think, what if I cannot use them again. I never think this. I think about how I never think this, and how great it is not to have to think such depressing thoughts. I see other people in therapy who will never lift their arms. Some are not so old. People who have fallen out of trees while climbing to retrieve a Frisbee on a summer afternoon, slipping and falling and ending up on the ground under the tree, now unplugged from the central nervous system, their brain wondering what happened, arms and legs indifferent, stick arms that say, well, this I how it's going to be now. Now we see how it is. What if I learn the swinging my arms into place, up onto my lap, onto a chair arm, onto a table is all there is? Gravity now means business. Jacob recommends several books about the weather. I get interested in the weather maps they show on Channel Nine during my white-soup dinners. Why do they make those concentric circles? What does it all mean? Does anyone watch the weather on TV and see those circles and get what they are talking about? Or have we all agreed not to know? I flip through books, find illustrations of something called the Coriolis Force. In a used copy of *Weather in Life Magazine Science Library,* the pictures dominate—old-timey black and white photos—showing how weather works. Men in Brylcreem and creased slacks stand to the side in these shots, pointing at maps and diagrams. The Coriolis Force is illustrated using an LP on a hi-fi. The camera is directly above the turntable so you can look down at the LP. From the spindle in the center are eight black strings. They spoke out from the spindle, then begin to curve like a nautilus shell as the LP turns. The curvature signifies the Coriolis Force, the effect of the spinning Earth, deflecting and steering all winds in general circulation. If the Earth did not spin, the winds would blow directly north to south, vice versa in the Southern Hemisphere. What would that world be like? I learn the Coriolis Force may not really be the most accurate nomenclature. More accurately an effect than a force. Effect designates something that necessarily and directly follows or occurs by reason of a cause. The Earth rotates out from under the moving air, introducing, voila, the effect called Coriolis, named for Gaspard-Gustave de Coriolis, the French mathematician who first described it.

So. Now we prepare for the prom, the cast ingeniously masked. I see that this is a miracle, as outfits go. My mother has outdone herself; I look as if I am getting better. The best part is the shoes, lavender espadrilles the exact color of the shimmering

Indian cotton blouse. God was with me on this shopping trip, she tells me. Downstairs my friend Jean waits; she will drive me to the prom for the thirty minutes or so before I get too tired and the burning pain begins to shoot down my left side. The piece of hip bone shaved off for the cervical spine graft makes its absence known. Pain defies words, I find. Hence the graphic language: burning, stabbing, sharp. You get caught up in it and it's like being entangled in a wind directed only at you, forcing you, pushing you, an effect only on you.

Jean and I drive over to The War Memorial, a Greek Revival public building overlooking the bright azure waters of Lake St. Claire. I do not have a rose corsage, something I really wanted but felt was the last thing I should be thinking about at a time like this. The War Memorial with its stepped terraces and ornate stone fences dividing carefully tended, artful gardens designed for strolls. The sky still bright as time edges closer to the solstice, the longest day of the year. The main ballroom almost dark, like some purple fairy dusk. I hear the Rolling Stones, Bob Seger, The Knack, the Electric Light Orchestra, Rod Stewart—guys from England and Michigan urging us to understand how they feel strange and lonely, searching for some place to call home. I don't really listen to the words, although I know them, will most likely always know them all. Jean leads me to a chair inside, set to one side of the dance floor in the midst of dozens of white-clothed tables, a chair set up for me—the person who needs a particular seat for her thirty-minute prom—a chair decorated with crepe paper. My legs are thin pegs, still tan from the holiday right before the accident. My closest friends are used to seeing me like this, but many others have trouble making their faces fit their smiling mouths.

Jean wanders off to find me a pop and I sit, alone for a moment, taking it all in. Black tuxedos are not the fashion this year, so the dance floor is pastel pairs, girls in slinky, butter yellow dresses, and boys in white or dove grey or pale blue tuxedos. The muted hues move with rock and roll songs and talk and look out floor-to-ceiling glass windows at the darkening blue of the lake, where freighters steam by, heading north from the Ford plant at River Rouge to Duluth to pick up taconite then bring it back to the ironworks where the ore pellets will be forged into Mustangs. They are long, straight, ships, the largest stretching to 1,000 feet. I see a ship sitting high in the water, empty, making way north toward Huron, Sault Ste. Marie, and then Superior.

My friend Peter sidles up to me, in a grey tuxedo and bright red face. His date, a girl named Greta, is a nut for Steve Martin. Martin has two schticks we all know: "I am a wild and crazy guy," and the "arrow through the head." Greta will not stop acting like the wild and crazy guy, Peter says, exasperated. I've just seen him hollering at her above the music: what is wrong with you? Do you think you are Steve Martin? Because I didn't want to come to the prom with Steve, got that. Or some wild and crazy guy. And I've seen her response, leaning back and waving her arms side to side over her head, exactly like some wild and crazy guy. So Pete takes my hand and heaves me gently up from the chair and escorts me onto the dance floor. It is a slow-fast song, "Night Moves," by Seger and we begin dancing together, holding hands, swaying. I forget that I cannot turn my head. I feel the push of the metal screws where the halo brace is held in place on my skull when I try to glance to my right or look at something specific. My arms behave little better than wet noodles. The hand that is not held flops at the end of an arm that is not strong enough to hold its own weight for more than an instant. It must look like some weird rag doll dance, but no one is watching. Pete tries to hide from Steve Martin; other couples bury themselves in the bear-hug style dancing we all favor. My hip begins to scream. I catch Pete's eye. Pete came to see me every day in the hospital. I look at him and he half lifts me, gently takes me toward a car and bed. Outside in the still, warm, June air, I look at the water. Small floating instances of radiant light crawl across the dark. Shining silver masts, crosses, and metal boughs blink as they slap across the water, sails down, waiting.

Jacob's right: Weather is a fun hobby. It says, see, it's real. How air moves. In the small weather book, a call to participate in understanding: Try these experiments, the author urges. What is more, a number of very interesting hours can be spent in experiments that will contribute to our understanding. No need for devices that will tax the pocketbook. Jacob, who sits in his garden and writes a stranger every day, writes of air and his wife of 42 years, now dead, and talks about glories. He says, I copied something from one of my books that might be of interest to you. You mentioned wearing a halo brace. I don't really know what this is, but I thought you would be interested in another type of halo, a glory. Glories are created when the sunlight is diffracted and scattered back toward the sun by water droplets in the clouds. You need to be up high to see these; above the clouds helps, because glories usually happen when the sun is when the sun is high above the horizon. People see them in the mountains and when flying in airplanes. Some hikers call glories 'mountain specters.' By the way, Jacob says, imagine this: When you see a glory, your shadow is often visible in the center of the rings, which alternate red and blue hues. I dream of glories lifted high in the air. Air. Air pressure, the weight of the atmosphere on a square centimeter or a single vertebra in your neck, is measured in millibars. A millibar is one one-thousandth of a bar or one thousand dynes per square centimeter. What does that mean now? Imagine curvilinear lines, called isobars: They describe gradations of air on a weather map, the way topographical maps describe elevation. Air with mass, pulled down by gravity, moves.

EPISODE SEVEN

My work comes first, reasons for it follow.—Andy Goldsworthy

The eye is astonished in contemplating the prodigious size of these trees . . . whose tufted summits were crowned with an ever verdant foliage: others, loosened by age from their roots, were supported by neighbouring trees, whilst, as they gradually decayed, they were incorporated . . . with the parent-earth . . . a striking picture of the operations of nature, who, left to herself, never destroys but that she may again create. (. . .) We were filled with admiration at the sight of these ancient forests, in which the sound of the axe had never been heard.—Jacques-Julien de Labillardière

July: On Blue Gums

The forest is a language, transmitting complex ideas through form. Who is writing this language? Of course it is God. I say this in conversation on a flight from San Francisco to Sydney, we are at 38,000 feet, and the listener is a scientist named Robert randomly assigned to the seat next to me. I am answering a question. Having lapped the globe about three and a half times solo, my experience is that speaking to seatmates at length on long flights is ill advised. However, this scientist is the exception to the rule. He is famous in his field, as it turned out, and tells an excellent story. He was returning from a conference at an Ivy League school on the East Coast and had stopped in the Bay Area to give a couple of invited talks. He wore a maroon cashmere sweater and wide-wale corduroy pants and told me how much he hated America. *But I like most of the Americans I meet,* he added. I told him I had hated Australian cities when I lived there because it felt so parochial but now it felt so much more diverse and alive. Better even than San Francisco.

When Robert finds out I teach at an art school and write about how people place themselves in a landscape. *He finds particular delight in both of these. (Why didn't I think of that question?* he asks. At first I think he is mocking me, and then I see he is not. He is serious and it makes me feel happy about the trip I am on, like the divine knew I needed some reassurance and is telling me I am on the right path.) He wants to know why artists stay in their studios when all the art and design action is found in woods, mountains, oceans. He wants to know why museums place art into windowless rooms and make it so separate. I tell him museum curators and archivists both seem to have a hint of revulsion for sharing their treasures. Robert agrees and adds that museums and libraries often behave more like conservative governments, defining rules around scarce resources and allowing access only to those who can pay. Robert is thinking about climate change and he wonders aloud when water will trump art, oil, gold, and silicone as the most coveted thing for all. Then the real wars will start, he intones.

They serve us our vegetarian meals, some sort of cauliflower curry with a spoonful of rice and a square of iced chocolate cake. Robert pressed the call button and orders a second gin and a white wine for me, like we are in some restaurant. The flight crew recognizes him and then serves us as though we are. He nibbles the curry and continues, *Wouldn't artists be better off spending as much time as they could outside every day and then painting for short periods of time, functioning more as transcribers than creators?* This is a good question. *It's all changing,* I say. *I feel like we should all drop everything and document it.* We touch plastic cups in a toast. *To documentation,* he says.

After dinner, Robert fell asleep with his mouth agape and I curled into the window seat. We were halfway to Sydney and the sky was a pale rose, the plane churning across its highest reaches. I love being on the top end of the sky.

My plane readings on Tasmanian native species were organized into clear folders, tabbed and labeled. The first thicker set covers research on logging interests and timber management in Tasmania and the history of the blue gum tree. The second set covers the actor Errol Flynn. He was from

Tasmania, too. In the still dark of the plane, I read *My Wicked, Wicked Ways,* Flynn's autobiography. I knew Flynn's films from when I was a kid. They would be on the UHF channels on weekend mornings, old timey, black and white, cowboys and Robin Hood and pirates. In real life, he was a character of his own design, a bon vivant and noted party boy—on Catalina Island off the California coast, he dug pits in the sand and roasted whole pigs, a Tasmanian tradition. He wrote like a scriptwriter for one of those films, with an eye towards quotes and the bon mot: "By instinct I am an adventurer; by choice I would like to be a writer; by pure unadulterated luck I am an actor." He also noted in what sounds ironic based on how he lived and what has been written about how he lived, "My job is to defy the normal." Flynn somehow salvaged his career as a swashbuckler and cowboy on the big screen after being accused of statutory rape in 1943 and acquitted. He had a home on Mulholland Drive, later revealed to include peepholes and a two-way mirror in the bathroom, installed at his command. I closed the book. Get me back to the trees, I say to no one.

I tried to spread information from the Australian Forestry Education Foundation on the tiny tray table. It is a tense story of when trees fail to triumph in the face of adversity. Tasmania, an island roughly the size of Ireland, is known equally in the twenty-first century for apples, wine, and tourism. But for many years, the economy of Tasmania was a timber economy and the forests were plundered. Tasmania is 125 miles south of Australia's southern coast. The Australian state retains a certain resonance as an outlaw environment, first as a notorious penal colony, then as a safe-haven for outlaws on the run from the mainland, then as a place largely controlled by logging interests. What I had learned through my research is that the history of Tasmania is a history of very old, very large trees with unusual qualities and amazing resilience, exploited for hundreds of years. Beginning in the nineteenth century, the worldwide demand for timber surged alongside ever-more mechanized methods for removing trees and creating lumber. In the 1850s,

steam power meant a dramatic spike in deforestation. By the
end of the nineteenth century, so many trees had been felled
for timber or burned to clear land for agriculture, the economy
shifted away from timber and towards industry. World War
I served as a catalyst for forest management in Tasmania.
Britain was intent on local production to protect its economy
after wars with major trading partners; a new sense of self-
sufficiency replaced the idea of world markets. The literature
also reported how toothless regulatory bodies failed to protect
the forests and how for much of the twentieth century rules
were unenforceable because of underfunded oversight agencies.
The loggers, I surmised, did whatever they wanted regardless of
the law because there was no one to stop them.

I fall asleep and awaken as the cabin lights spring on and
a chipper voice on the PA states we are on final approach to
Sydney. *Cabin crew, take your seats.* I am blanketed in tree
information. Robert is sipping a coffee, and he tells me I look
like some sort of art installation. We part ways   **Hobart Airport**

after customs: He tells me to write and tell him what I think of Tasmanian apples, which he claims are the best in the world.

Five or ten hours later—time compresses and expands on these long hauls, on a wildly clear June morning, I step off a small jet in Hobart, Tasmania's capital. I have been traveling for 27 hours, and this time in pressurized tubes imbues the world with a psychedelic effect. The air in the high southern latitudes, unsullied by pollution, puts a sharp lens on the outlines of land against sky, water reflects all with perfect clarity. This is how the entire world was before we started burning whatever we could find to burn, trees being first on the list. I take a deep breath in, and the cool, clean air revives me after the long flight.

At my wharf-side hotel, a brick and mortar renovated jam factory named for the jam magnate Henry Jones, I drop off my bags and immediately walk out to take in the view. Kunanyi/Mount Wellington in English, Unghbanyahletta or Poorawetter in Aboriginal, at 4,000 feet it is the summit of the Wellington Range. Hobart is built onto the Wellington Range's foothills. I turn and look the other way, and the water is so clear—it reminds me of Antarctica, how it mirrors perfectly the lightly snow-touched mountain. It is June, so winter in Hobart, and the weather is crisp.

I thought about this as I watched trucks stacked with shaved-naked tree trunks head for the port. They were heading for the wood chipper. I had seen the statistics across the twentieth century—how from 1947 to 1957 the volume of sawn timber cut from Tasmanian native forests had doubled, because of the post-war housing boom. The wood chip industry in Tasmania emerged in the 1960s. Particle and fiberboards were replacing timber as building materials because the quality of glues and adhesives improved. This allowed the "forest waste"—trees, branches, and other bits not suitable as saw logs—to be sold as product, too. Then the Japanese got involved. Interestingly, this wood chip business is told as a story that eased excessive logging. But. Then the wood chip industry accelerated wildly and became highly controversial. By 1974, more than a million tons of wood chips were exported each year. If you want to visualize that amount, think of it being the equivalent mass of 333,000 Orcas, or 200,000 adult elephants.

My Tasmanian research journey had two agendas: First, I was speaking at the University of Tasmania, which was hosting the humanities and social sciences special interest group of the Scientific Committee on Antarctic Research. Then I was going to place my hands on some of the largest specimens of eucalyptus in the world. Since I first learned of the Presidio eucalyptus trees' ties to Tasmania, I had longed to touch them. I wanted to feel the cold southern air that nourished them, to smell their scent in that clean air, and to hear the wind move leaves and dangling bark against ginormous trunks. Place beckons or summons me as a sensual experience, and then I simply must go and feel it, hear it, taste it for myself.

About 100 Antarctic humanities researchers largely from the U.S., Australia, New Zealand, and the UK with a few continentals thrown in talked The Ice for three days. One night we all boarded large coaches and headed to the House on a hill, a stately home built by convicts where liveried officers greeted us and escorted us to the top of a grand staircase where we were then announced. It was like being in a movie, and Errol Flynn flickered across my mind. I walked carefully down the steps and accepted a small glass of whiskey from a silver tray then joined a circle of polar explorers, sharing news from The Ice. The next day, I spoke about Antarctic diaries and vernacular photography, and the role of "simple seamen" in exploration and how we could also know the Antarctic through unofficial stories. I liked to show what I found in archives written by the crews, the diaries and the letters; these men are generally silenced, their hours and years of experiences left to languish in musty journals and stacks of photographs shoved in boxes in archives, or under beds in small towns in New Zealand, Ireland, Canada, and the UK. Hundreds of people are in this research group, tucked into universities and colleges or working as solo artists or researchers.

When the conference ended, I loaded my backpack into the boot of a small rental car. My first stop was the town of

Geeveston, then on to the Tahune AirWalk. I followed the A6 southwest toward the Huon Valley. The road away from Hobart loops along, and I was often the only vehicle on the road. It was a bright, sunny day, and the city became hills covered with curving lines of orchards. Soon I saw an untended farm stand, wooden crates filled with bags of apples. A small signed explained the pricing and how money was to be tucked into a small slot. I thought of the scientist as I selected a bag; it was the stuff of a Cézanne—the apples were neither too large nor too scrawny, vivid crimson flecked with bright green. I drove along munching on an apple and recalling how delicious the apple is—how good they taste when they are not so very long off the tree, almost like tasting the tree that made them.

What a strange and beautiful place Tasmania is—how the environment is designed in a sense by water, because sea levels began rising about 12,000 years ago and 6,000 years into this rise, Tasmania was separated from the Australian continent and became an island. Darwin stopped in on the *Beagle* and celebrated his twenty-seventh birthday in Hobart. In isolation unique locals, both fauna and flora, evolved, the Tasmanian devil, about the size of a small dog, and the largest carnivorous marsupial on the planet; the pandani, the largest heath plant in the world; and of course, the ginormous eucalyptus trees.

The Forest and Heritage Centre in Geeveston was described by someone in Hobart as an unofficial tourist office for the local timber history. Before leaving Hobart, I had coffee and donuts in a quaint café with one of my Antarctic colleagues, an artist from Sydney; she listened to my plan to drive into the forest and warned: *Do not tell any one you meet that you used to go to sea with Greenpeace and don't talk about environmental issues. Full stop. Don't even tell them your real name. Make up a name: You are Sally, and you are a primary school teacher from Wisconsin.* When she said Wisconsin, we both laughed. She was not being a scold or hysteric. I had reported on environmental issues and knew what she meant. People get agitated about place: Changing them or stopping people from changing them.

She explained, *The whole economy down there blew up in the 1980s when one of the timber mills closed, and they are—what do you call them? Red necks in general. They are all pro-timber.*

Geeveston has a distinctly timber-tourist aesthetic— Tasmanian crafts, Tasmanian wood—as though the only people who came through were tourists looking to buy things carved from local trees. The Forest and Heritage Centre is one big ad for wood production. It told of the Geeves family who founded the town and of the larger Tasmanian timber industry. I wandered the forestry centre alone, and the teenager at the desk spoke into a tiny mobile phone about whether she should braid her hair for a party that evening. She did not look up. The video screens, touted as offering a discussion of forestry management, stared out in black silence.

There was actually a lot not to like about Geeveston, a place with a self-congratulatory message around tree exploitation and profiteering. *Get me out of here,* I said under my breath.

I then drove towards Big Arve, a tree about 10 kilometers outside of town. It was advertised as the easiest big tree to get to—with a "sealed road all the way." I parked near one other car and walked the last 50 meters.

Big Arve defies language, but I guess majestic will do for now. The base of the trunk, and continuing up about two storeys, is a thick brown bark that then stops and is replaced by shimmery beige and green trunk. I stood there, mouth agape, like an idiot, staring up. There was an Australian family nearby, and they had the same reaction: *Roit? Roit? Wasn't I roit it was worth the detour?* The father appealed his children.

The tree somehow survived what are known as the Black Tuesday Bushfires of 1967, when 110 separate fires burned across the island, killing sixty-two people and destroying thousands of structures. The fires were caused by a particular collision of typical weather conditions—low humidity, high temperatures, and high winds. The fire that raged through the Huon Valley killed other large, old trees, but Big Arve survived. It is a *eucalyptus regnans,* the eucs that are among the largest trees on the planet, and stands at 87 meters in height (imagine an American football field standing on its end) and is described as holding 360 cubic meters of wood. The story is strange—how loggers knew of Big Arve in the 1950s, then the fire, then the tree was "discovered" in the 1980s and given a protected status.

After readjusting my sense of scale and just taking photos for a while, when the loud family left, I told the tree how I had come from San Francisco and how other genera there were thriving and loved. I explained 300 acres of trees are in the Presidio—many of them Monterey pine, Monterey cypress, and eucalyptus. The eucalyptus is the variety called Tasmanian blue gum, *Eucalyptus globulus,* considered non-native species yet participate in the Presidio ecosystem in a remarkable way. The trees embrace and repurpose fog as ground water, distributing it into the soil, to be shared by all in the forest. I believe this news from faraway made Big Arve happy, and I also believe it is not a good idea to anthropomorphize nature. And yet I talk to trees. Perhaps this makes sense in that I don't think of trees as partially human, like the trees in *The Wizard of Oz.* I think of them as communicative and senscient, from the Latin *sintere* to feel. I think the trees can feel me like I feel them.

The day turns grey, the sky heavy, as I wend my way towards the Tahune AirWalk. The road is lined with signs, "Big Tree Lookout, previous stop." Tasmania is a science-fictional landscape where, left to its own devices, the flora decided to go big. Huge ferns, eucalyptus regnans, and then the air filled with the distant buzzing or whir of machines, akin to what I have heard in 1960s sci-fi films, the sound the giant ants make before they emerge from beyond the sand dunes. There are signs asking me to share the road with the large logging trucks. The radio stations are hard to find, and dreadful music squawks out when tuned in.

The AirWalk opened in 2001, and its combination of easy hikes, zip lines and gift shop/café tucked alongside a World Heritage-listed forest have made it one of the most popular tourism destinations in Tasmania, a sign told me. I did not research the competition for this distinction. The place was packed and the road lined with buses, the car park almost full. Not what I had been expecting for a winter weekday in southern Tasmania. I stopped in the café for a sandwich and some tea and saw they had pitchers of a yellow drink—lemonade?—lined up for free.

I asked the clerk what it was.

Oh! That's water. That's the water from the Huon River.

Yellow?

Yea. From the tree tannins. Nothing to harm you. Tastes fine. Have a try.

I poured myself a glass of the yellow water and it tasted a little odd, but I could not really be sure whether it was my mouth or my eyes telling me that. Somehow I could not bring myself to drink it. I sipped my milky Earl Grey tea instead.

After my sandwich, I wandered around the building. A quilt made by the Southern Spinners and Craft Group and the Huon Valley Quilters caught my eye. The quilters had taken walks in the forest for creative inspiration for the intricate forest scene. The sky and mountain range were hand-painted on homespun cotton fabric, then tree bark was used to create a fallen log covered with embroidered lichen and fungi.

One of the AirWalk clerks stopped as I stared at the quilt and listed all the flora depicted: *ferns, panda, laurel, sassafras, leatherwood, silver wattle, lichens, fungi, waratahs, gum top stingy bark, dianella, blackwood—and blue gum.*

I head out for a short loop walk to check out the famed Huon Pines, which are native to the region and are some of the Earth's oldest species. I take out my notebook and write down the location of the AirWalk. Walking amidst the laurel, the gum—signs attached to trees talking about what they are good for—ships, for instance, flooring in Japan! I find this startling. What we make trees into has no place here in the woods. As I walk along, the winter gloaming settles on the rainforest, the air is cooler, the sky deeper grey, and I gaze at two rivers converging, the Huon and the Picton, and both are the color of root beer from tree tannins.

LAT: 43° 5'42.34"S
LON: 146°43'47.00"E

The Huon Pine reminds me how easy it is to get fixated on a thing—in my case the blue gum and other eucs—and thus miss the magical in my immediate gaze. *Lagarostrobus franklinii*—comes from two Greek words, *lagaros*, thin, and *strobos,* cone. The species name franklinii honors Sir John Franklin, who was the lieutenant-governor of Tasmania from 1836–1843—and whose name is indelibly chiseled into polar adventure lore for sailing off to discover the Northwest Passage, never to return, and prompting decades of speculation and search parties. (A journey, incidentally, where, in addition to losing 129 human lives, two great historic wooden Antarctic exploration ships *Terror* and *Erebus* were lost as well.) *Lagarostrobus franklinii* has been posited to be the oldest tree species in Australasia, with some stands in Tasmania dated to 3,000 AD and sediments found in a lake dated to 10,500 years old. Among conifers, I later read, this is the longest period of continued persistence of unique genetic material.

Huon Pine is dubbed the Prince of Tasmanian Timbers. It has a golden color, a rich distinct perfume, a high oil content, a fine grain, and is an ideal boat-building material. It grows along rivers and lakes, generally preferring to have its roots, or feet, in the water. It is Australia's oldest species and painfully slow growing, taking 1,000 years to reach a height of 30 meters. In contrast with eucs, the *lagarastrobus franklinii* has taken a very focused path around adaptation—or lack thereof. I look at the drooping, light-green foliage, tiny leaves, almost more scales than leaves, all in a spiral pattern on twiggy pieces. It has a gentle, wistful form.

I head to the town of Franklin and stop in at the Aqua Grill. The water in Franklin is neither yellow nor brown, to my relief. After a meal of salt-and-pepper calamari, chips, salad, and sauvignon blanc, I have a flat white and admire the small town.

Very twee. It skirts the Huon River amidst rolling, tree-covered hills. I wandered down to Village Antiques, where I unearthed some framed, embroidered post cards from World War I. The girls in France would use silk thread to embroider missives for Australian and American and other foreign soldiers to send home—Kind Thoughts or Thinking of You. They are delicate and while their silk threads are faded and the linen is yellowed, I buy them and tuck them carefully into my bag.

Back at my hotel, I write about the day, the Huon Pine, then turn out the light and listen as the vast nocturnal army of marsupials begins doing their thing in the bush. Tasmania is an ecosystem very much attuned to darkness and as I drifted off to sleep, I wondered how that choice came to be made by its inhabitants—that the night was for living and hunting, and the day was for resting far from the sun's glare.

The next day, I drive towards Hastings then on to Kettering and take the ferry to Bruny Island. It is 1 degree Celsius as I wait to drive aboard the car ferry. Penguins adorn the side of the ferry, in honor of the local fairy or little penguins, *eudyptula minor,* a species increasingly impacted by climate change as rising ocean temperatures alter their habitats' ecosystems and cats and dogs pester and attack them on land. It is a clear sky, no clouds, and the sea is a flat, navy blue. Next to me in the car line, a Hilux truck with a sheep in the back, tied up. The sheep has the vacant, stupid expression of its species, and I watch as a tall man in another car talks to it. *Look how sad you are,* he says, in a loud American voice. Soon you'll be free. The man is an idiot, and I am happy he is not traveling with me. I call out, *I think they are taking it to the slaughter-house.* The man looks at me, alarmed. The driver of the truck is no where to be found. I get out of my car and climb the stairs, topside, to stand up by the wheelhouse as we make the short crossing.

I have booked a place at Morella on the island, offering a view north towards Adventure Bay, where Cook, Bligh, and d'Entrecasteaux all rested on their long, exploratory journeys, prowling the high seas for treasures.

Before I check in, I drive around the island stopping to buy local cheese, oysters, and wine. The oysters from Bruny Island are famous in Australia.

A window at Morella on Bruny Island

They are briny and huge, feeding in the cold clean waters of the d'Entrecasteaux Channel. In small places like Bruny with limited access, it is guaranteed you will run into the same people and sure enough, Sheep Man is there. He is buying a T-shirt that says "Get Shucked!" from the café shop and making loud comments about oysters and sex. His partner, a small, tan blonde, has a pained look on her face. I sense this might be their last trip together. Her gaze has shifted away and is relaxed and focused on the water.

I eat a dozen on the spot, chatting with the oyster folks about their lives. Pretty quiet, they tell me. They are all locals. No desire to be or go anywhere else. They all want to know if I have loved the Tahuni AirWalk. I get another dozen oysters to go. At Morella I check into a room that has a rounded wall of glass and is called the Cockpit. There's a wood fire and an outdoor hot tub, and I set a fire and grill some local ODO (one day-old) cheese on rosemary sultana bread over the logs.

That night, I sit by the cast-iron stove and read from Jacques-Julien Houto de Labillardière's exploration of Recherche Bay. On May 6, 1792, Labillardière made what he called his most noteworthy discovery and had a Tasmanian Blue Gum felled to collect the flowers. The enormous size dazzled the crew and they immediately saw the shipbuilding potential in the tall, straight trunks. His carpenters used Blue Gum to raise the gunwhales on their oared landing boats. The blue is part of the myrtle family, *Myrtaceae*—a group that thrives both in drought-prone areas and in tropical rainforests. The tree is named for its flowers—which are strewn across the roads and trails of the Presidio —derived from the Greek, *eu*—meaning true or well—and *calyptus*—meaning cap or cover. The flower is designed so that the cap pops off, revealing a flower and a shallow cup that holds nectar.

Surrounding this nectar are long, silken white stamen. Once pollinated, the stamen falls away and a nut-like fruit develops. As they ripen and slowly dry out, these woody lozenges sway with branches before finally taking flight, hurled by the Pacific winds. The second cap covering the lozenge gives way, and seeds are released.

By 1905, the blue gum was the tree by which the entire species was known, and four million feet were supplied to the British Admiralty for wharf piles. More than 1.3 million hectares of blue gum or *Eucalyptus globulus* are planted around the world in the twenty-first century. I know that blue gums first came to California in the late 1800s; people were looking for forests that were fast-growing and offered useful timber.

I put my book down, and sifted through my bags for Forest Talk, a government information sheet about Tasmanian forests. By 2008, forty-three percent of the state of Tasmania had been placed into its reserve system. Almost eighty percent of the old growth forest was today on reserved land. I watched the flames nourished by some tree, thinking of Big Arve, miraculously escaping axe and fire, rediscovered, protected, its shiny-silvered-tangled trunk so artistic, better than anything in a museum. Robert from the plane will enjoy hearing this reflection, I think. I make a note to send my review of the apples and to include a shot of the tree with its hopeful story.

NOTEBOOK SEVEN

I do not know where this journey ends. Otherwise why call this action journey.—Matsuo Bashō

As the pilot announced we were making our final approach to Hobart Airport, someone yells out, *I can't see the airport.* Someone else calls back, *Who cares, mate, you're not the bloody pilot.*

I see the mighty Southern Ocean, glowing five shades of sapphire and then a thin twist of yellow sand. There is indeed no sign of an airport, and we are at about 1,000 feet or so. I hear his panicked voice and felt vaguely irritated. I come and go with flying fears. But on this day I am once again the fearless me who left America in 1987 to explore the world as a news reporter and writer, the me who flies around the world solo and who rarely panicked about turbulence even while flying on little-known airlines in faraway places on craft that had seen better days. That me was too busy being thrilled with it all—checking the board that clicked over destinations, a sound and event that always made me stop and consider how many of us were on the road at that very moment, surging into the clouds and into some new adventure. As we roll up to the small Hobart airport, I smile. *On the road again.*

Later that night, I am at Smolt in Hobart—a lovely bistro in Salamanca Square. Surreal for my space-and-time transplanted head and body. I can see I am in a bistro and can read the menu and order wine and food and yet I know my brain is still parked back over the ocean. By morning, it will have caught up. The wall-sized fish tank enhances a sense of capsular separation from the rest of the world by cognitive dislocation. Feeling observant of surroundings yet all feels projected, virtual.

Later still that night, I cannot sleep. Give up pretending to sleep. Begin to write about what's on my mind: Waves. The wave pattern in nature, as sound wave, light wave, and ocean wave. Jean-Baptiste Joseph Fourier is credited with first seeing that any periodic function can be broken into a series of (even infinite) simple oscillating functions and with thinking through ideas of how atmospheric gases could become trapped and heated (to be later named, "the greenhouse effect.")

If the only form is a wave.

If the only form is a sine wave.

If you ponder the most basic form as an equation.

Finally, I fall asleep, the strange deep and shallow sleep of jet lag. The dream world is akin to a wildlife show and I am the narrator and the host. Sunlight fills the forest. I head north-northeast, skirting the campground where no one camps most of the year, across an installation called Presidio Habitats and then watch, amazed, as a red-tail hawk, *buteo Jamaicensis* buzzes me, holding a struggling mole in its mouth. The mole is doomed—soon to be breakfast. And yet it thrashes on—getting its first and only feel of life above the Earth's surface, clearly not enjoying the ride and fresh perspective. These hawks have eyes evolved to focus in on the Earth's surface from 100 feet or so. What chance could a plump mole have, thinking the coast is clear, to find, yikes, the swift, stocky bird. If the mole were smaller, the hawk would eat her whole. If she were a fellow bird, her head would be ripped off, then she would be eaten. The mole is in the unfortunate position to require a technique where it will be killed via talon. I have seen photographs of small mammals after they have fallen into a red-tail hawk's possession, and the result is a harsh scene. The hawk simply rips them to pieces, bit by bit, eating as they go. This wild nature is excruciating in actual fact for me. I awaken in the dark, bathed in a light sweat, trying to make out where I am. I check my phone and ninety minutes have passed since I turned out the light. It is going to be a long night.

"The subject of the introduction of the eucalyptus as a sanitary agency in fever-stricken countries has of late been so much talked about that some authoritative preliminary inquiries have been made with the view of planting Eucalyptus globulus on a large scale in Mauritius."—*Nature,* June 11, 1874, p. 112.

" . . . the Italian government, following the course that it has already adopted on previous occasions, will gratuitously distribute this year 5,000 plants of the Eucalyptus globulus, for cultivation in the Agro Romano, especially in the spot infected by malaria."—*Nature,* April 1, 1875, p. 436.

The highest point in the Presidio is Rob Hill, 384 feet. It is five minutes from my front door. Rob Hill campground big renovation in 2008–09, and while it was closed, watercolor sketches posted at the site showed the new, improved camp with a stone shelter and views; improved trail links the camp ground to the beach.

If I look past the stack of books, Munari, Abbey, Proust, Eiseley, Shonagon, Basho, Woolf, old friends from faraway, out the sliding window in my bedroom, an ugly metal frame corroded by salt air, past the cypress trees' dead and dangling branches, past the red and cream, then newly painted grey and green, apartments at the bottom of the dunes, then out over the abandoned battery fixed up to be a walkers' destination, past the stubby light-house with no name, past Lands End to the Pacific, I see the Farallon Islands, a place name from the Spanish, meaning pillar or cliff.

If I think about how not so very long ago in geologic terms, I could've walked to those pillars or cliffs we call Farallon Islands because they were connected to where I sit by land, not separated by water.

If I think about melting and wonder, hey, what will I not be able to walk to around here in 10,000 years, or what will some latest version of life be doing in this space in 9,999 years, or 999 years or 99 years or nine years?

And how about if I think about when people stop walking, they will also stop writing, because writing and walking are the same thing. Technologies created by humans to adapt to the absorption and transfer of information.

Both invite trespassing into marked-off terrains, wandering into the unknown, exploring a white expanse called page or screen, or a forest or ice cap.

A sign in New Zealand:
We only preserve what we love
We only love what we understand
We only understand what we study

Latitude 37 degrees 49 minutes 46 seconds North, 122 degrees 31 minutes 24 seconds West.

A cold, clear, blustery afternoon in the Headlands, at home in the Headlands Center for the Arts. The room has two high windows, four panes each, each pane the size of a doormat. I begin by finding true north on my compass.

I push these thoughts out of my head and turn to a page on my desk, a page that says, *pinus radiata*. Pinus radiata: The poetics of fact. Pine trees lived along the California coast in the Quarternary—but fared poorly under Holocene conditions. There is fossil evidence that pine trees lived in the Northern California headlands, the land we call the Presidio, before the trees brought in by Major Jones et al. A small book called *Pacific Coast Tree Finder*—a pocket arborist—a staple-bound pocket manual for identifying Pacific Coast trees. There are five symbols in the book to describe the sorts of places Pacific Coast trees may grow:

- **Warm, sunny ridges**
- **Stream banks or in soggy soil**
- **Seacoast trees**
- **Burned areas**
- **Abandoned farmyards, etc**

It offers a series of small isotypes designed to help see the trees for the forest. See. See the. See the trees. See the trees for the forest.

Note taped to my door:

There are a few tree swings in your neighborhood. The Presidio Trust's Forestry crew has informed us that tree swings have a negative impact, since they bind the tree, creating a dangerous condition over time by weakening limbs.

Tree swings are located near building 1433. If a swing belongs to you, please remove it no later than Friday, December 16. If you need assistance in safely removing the swing, the Presidio Trust will be happy to help. Please call the work order desk at 561.4270 for assistance.

Any swing left after December 16 will be removed

Thank you for your cooperation.

EPISODE EIGHT

August: On Remediation

The serpentine bluffs loom over Baker Beach, which faces due west and where on clear days the Farallon Islands are seen in sharp relief, knife edges between the sea and sky. Baker Beach is well-known to the world; it is used as backdrop for many advertisements for San Francisco—travel, banking, cuisine. All captured and messaged in that one beach with the unobstructed views. Anyone can easily call it to mind: Think of the stretch of dark sand with the red bridge in the background, scrubby bluffs rising on the right side of the frame, the hills of Marin across the strait called Golden Gate, the blue Pacific on the left.

For decades, the U.S. Army used these bluffs as a dump, and the dump then became another pocket of a rather complex landscape restoration in the Presidio. The bluffs, which I can see from my back yard, are a ten-minute walk from my front door, and I get there by walking first down a sandy set of steps, then skirting the road's shoulder. While they are being cleared out and cleaned up, I spend time each day observing the process, taking a break to pick up my children after school. The operation is an intense sprint, twelve hours a day, six days a week and covers four months.

It has been a run of rainy winter days in San Francisco, and there is a brief break in the clouds, pale slivers of blue woven like so many silk ribbons through the putty-colored clouds. This is the routine: I stop writing to go get the children; in exchange, they come with me and help with the shopping.

Traffic is light, and the distance we cover small: San Francisco is a small city, only seven miles by seven miles. We are less than a couple of miles from each of their schools. I am relieved to settle into our Presidio home. We moved a lot in the past six years, from San Francisco to Iowa where I worked on an MFA in writing, to New Zealand where I was a Fulbright Fellow, to Iowa where I taught in the Honors College, then back to San Francisco where the other half of the biological family is: The fathers. Yes, to further complicate this, I had two children with two different men. When we travel and start at new places, when we fly, I answer the same questions: Why do you all have different last names? The amount of time I spend explaining why we have different last names is its own story.

We have finally settled down in our rented townhouse in the Presidio, a former military base on the northern edge of the city being rehabbed for civilian uses. This is our first school year together, all three of us, in two years. First, we three moved to Iowa for three years, so I could do the MFA, but my son had come back to San Francisco to be with his father after two years, but my daughter stayed with me; then we moved in two waves for the Fulbright to New Zealand. First my daughter and I were together in New Zealand, and then my son came; then he went back to San Francisco to live with his father again, and I moved back to Iowa with my daughter to teach for a year at the university. Then we moved back to San Francisco and restarted a version of the life we had before we left.

Dumps fascinate me. The fact there is one so close by lights me up in a particular way. I spring from bed in the morning, peer down the hill, mug of hot tea in hand, and watch as the crew starts work. Most days, it is just the slow and steady work of remediation. Then, there are the "stop everything" days, when they find ordnance and have to secure it and then blow it up in place. The ordnance dates from the Civil War, eight-inch cannon balls and eight-inch armor piercing shells for the Rodman rifle. However, most days the finds are everyday items, horseshoes, rubble, household bits and pieces.

When I head out mid-morning, the Presidio bluffs are soggy from five days of rain, but with a break in the weather, clouds moving across a blue sky, the spider excavators fairly jump off a flat-bed truck and get to work, clawing into moist chocolate soils. I wander down to the bluffs and watch the excavators claw away, settling in with a metal thermos of green tea and a thin Swiss cheese sandwich wrapped in wax paper. As their name implies, spider excavators have stabilizing legs, a compact center cabin where the human operator sits, and long, reaching claws.

I feel a sense of awe over their design and function, in part because of my son's younger days of singular devotion to construction sites and in part because they are the construction-machine analog of my own writing practice as an essayist. Writing is about memory, picking at something seen and recalled, figuring out why I am thinking about it, making decisions about how deep to dig. Writing work is a construction site of the mind, unearthing and building stories lurking in even the most mundane activity. A walk in London. Eating an oyster. A salt-water farm. And after writing these stories, the world is a different place for me, parsed with a new set of connections, evolved from readings and research and scribbling.

The Presidio bluffs remediation is theater, with all the unpredictability of an improvisational approach. On one of the "stop everything" days, they unearth ordnance (cannon balls) and have to close the road while they remove it; there is also the revelation that the site is contaminated with polycyclic aromatic hydrocarbon, or PAH. In the official reports, PAH is referred to as a potential chemical of concern, or PCOC.

While I was in still Iowa packing up and getting ready to move back to California, I had a friend help by driving by and seeing what a street or neighborhood was like. I noticed the Presidio was being adapted for civilians; and it was under market value. It was appealing because we could be in the city and also have a feeling of being wholly in nature. My drive-by buddy said the Presidio apartments were poorly maintained, but the cars were new and the place had what he called a "family vibe." I signed a lease with the Presidio, and we move in a month later.

The Presidio has a particular homesteading quality in these early years. We lose power a lot during winter storms. In contrast, we are surrounded by the wealthiest neighborhoods, and the local grocery stores are expensive. And the public schools stink, so both of my kids attend private schools. And yet in the midst of all this, I remain optimistic. I am completing my book on the Antarctic, and I am finding freelance work in writing and editing. And there is something optimistic about living in a new national park that is being renovated and remediated each month. Each week reveals something new, and most of these revelations are cause for delight and hope. Native plants are given a new chance to survive as trees are removed from the hill below our house; sick and dying trees are removed and replaced with young, healthy descendants of their species.

As I negotiate the narrow aisles of one of the expensive grocery stores, cringing at the prices for apples and milk but putting them in my cart anyway, others doing the same thing and I hear them talking to children, telling them to keep up, to pick cereal, to find the pineapples. It is obvious most of the other women in the store are the nannies. This did not take long for me to clue into at the grocery store, carpooling to soccer practice, at the renovated Julius Kahn Playground. I seem to be the only parent around on weekdays; so it is me and the nannies, the Hispanic women in white pants, the Norwegian and French nannies in bright green socks and sandals, and the "taking a break from college guy" who cheerfully tries to teach some five-year-old how to hold a lacrosse stick.

My children choose to wait in the car. They are no longer interested in coming into the market so they sit in the car, staring at small video game devices or a book, offhandedly asking me to come back with a fresh baguette. They have been supremely adaptable in all of these moves, taking on the new schools and the new places and getting into new teams. I will never be able to thank them enough, and I indulge them as reward.

I load the bags into the trunk of my aging car, and as I open the door, they both look at me with some disdain. What took you so long? Why did you go to the store after you picked us up? Why don't you go to the store in the morning, when we are in school? Waiting in the car is so boring! I smile.

We drive the short distance into the Presidio. From the curving road, you can see Alcatraz and beyond that Marin County across the choppy green waters of the bay. At home we unload our car, and the children vanish into their rooms to engage in some version of homework. I head out for my afternoon patrol of the bluffs.

Walking to the site, I recalled how in Antarctica I sat for hours one day with one of the strangest dumps on the planet. It was an open-cast pit, filled with office furniture, odd metal bits, papers, boxes, and plastic bins, and it smoldered. It exuded a weird, steady stream of smoke into an otherwise clear sky. Military dumps are jammed with pollutants including ordnance, toxins, chemicals and at that time the U.S. Navy was on duty in that part of the Antarctic. There are heavy metals, varied industrial waste, and I learn there are also the most complex molecules found in space to date, polycyclic aromatic hydrocarbons.

At home in the evening, after dinner and television and tucking-in time with the children, I pause with the PAH. I learn it is in tarry substances naturally found in coal and crude oil, the sources of the local PAHs. PAHs forms in the combustion of carbonaceous fuels and are found in auto exhaust, cigarettes, charred meat, and candle soot. While they have been fingered as a cause of cancer, they are also the largest and most complex molecules found in space, where they are entirely interwoven with dust, formed in the outflow of dying or evolving stars.

PAHs apparently mark a trail to a rare type of star, a trail that leads to the origin of life's building blocks. I read another short piece about PAHs that states, "There is evidence that huge quantities of PAHs exist in deep space, from the infrared light they emit, and amino acids have been found in meteorites landing on Earth. Organic molecules like these must have rained down on the early Earth, and may have helped life to begin." Polycyclic aromatic hydrocarbons also possess long-term stability, which is how the material can hurl through space and arrive intact on Earth and how they can be tipped into an Army dump and be exhumed decades later in fine form. (This is why they are called particularly important pollutants.) In reading about PAHs, I come across the spectroscopic fingerprint, the idea has a form and presence.

Over the next few weeks, my mind wanders towards PAHs and I read articles about what scientists who study them say and think, many of which I squint to understand. Contaminants can easily occupy my mind if I allow them to do so. When we were in Iowa, a notice would arrive with the water bill, as the snow thawed and melted; children two and under should not consume the tap water during this period. It was too contaminated with farm chemicals. After that first notice, I looked at water differently, as something vectoring in lethal chemicals. I stocked the house with enormous glass bottles of water—water for pasta, water for steaming vegetables, water for tea. I only used the tap for washing dishes and bathing. I did not know how to solve the bathing issue, skin being the body's largest organ and dermal absorption being possible, so I cut bathing times from relaxing soaks to rapid hose-downs.

As I read across scientific literature, I learn that while the source for the complex molecules called PAHs is uncertain, a leading researcher named Adolf Witt argued that they originated in space, in particular a place called the Red Rectangle. At the core of the nebula is a star about the mass of the Sun, but far older, I read that it is going through a brief turbulent stage; convection currents dislodge carbon-rich material from deep within the star as it nears the end of its life. Carbon and hydrogen then get caught up in the stellar wind and blown out to form the nebula, and as the gas cools, atoms collide to form larger and larger molecules. "The discovery of anthracene and pyrene is strong evidence that this process is really happening. And these two molecules are almost certainly far from the biggest being built in the Red Rectangle. There is no limit—eventually this will form particles of a million atoms or more," Witt told *New Scientist*. We are looking into a factory for organic molecules.

More than 70,000 tons of debris were pulled loose and moved by the spider excavators by November. This was moved 250 feet along the tops of the cliffs and disposed of; then a trail called Battery to Bluffs was constructed that allowed people to walk or stop and rest their bodies as they gazed westward.

I think about how we can make PAHs and how PAHs can find us from distant stars, how they make us and kill us, and I am again left feeling like a liquid in need of a mold to pour myself into. Instead, I start drawing.

So. The opacity of place, all the insoluble mysteries of each place. What comes to mind as I sketch and abstract this stereoscopic fingerprint from outer space, my 4B pencil allowing soft, wide lines of circles then messily filled in—are how Tolstoy—and Socrates before him—reminded us that all we can know is that we know nothing. What this place, this Presidio landscape, speaks to me about is how there are signs and wonders—an openness to ideas of life, survival, and knowledge that are both challenge and inspiration.

NOTEBOOK EIGHT

In 2009, as the redesign of the Presidio continued, benches and a walkway were built into the edge of the woods overlooking the cemetery. The cemetery is strangely beautiful in its design, the sharp lines of the white tombstones, the vivid lawn, the Golden Gate and red bridge in the distance.

The benches sit amidst a stone walkway and wall and the words of the Archibald MacLeish poem "The Young Dead Soldiers Do Not Speak" are carved into this display.

They have a silence that speaks for them at night and when the clock counts. They say, "We were young. We have died. Remember us."

Do you think it's easy to get those lines to look so fine? To look like there is intent in how we bury our dead. And what would those dead folk say, if they had teeth and tongues and soft palettes (and had not been consumed by worms and water and dark.) Would they find their fate ironic? Would they find their fate even mildly amusing? That here, right now, right down the hill from their final resting place we have a building called House of Air and in this place, children jump on canvas stretched tight. Jump. Scream. Twist. So many cinders hurled aloft towards a fossil sky.

When the colonists arrived, stirred and pushed by the beckoning winds, to find some other place, there were many souls who lived on these lands. The archeologists today find people here then—and these people are not in the cemetery and the tombstones ripple across the hills even in death they are the ones who are remembered. Costanoan. Ohlone. Some of the things they designed and made survive. They are in museums or found as so many fragments by archeologists who on some days are accompanied by school children or volunteers, educating themselves about what came before and how we dig with our hands to find it. The other souls who walked here melted into the soils and air. Come look for us, they say, we remain in here, where you walk.

The gun emplacements buried in the mist.

The smell of fog a mix of smoke and decay and water keeps the people away. When the rains come the path will melt into slick mud but for today, the sand is dry and covered with fine gravel and all is brittle. Merely lost in the fog. I cannot see the blue-tailed skink or the red-winged hawk or the mole. All lost to the tangle of grey air. The fog is a sort of miracle, the sort of effect I wouldn't really believe if I did not live in it, feel it, walk into it. When did I first see the fog? On television, as men emerged from graveyards with black hats and coats and canes or umbrellas. How they got it all wrong! No, the fog is more like God, it is everywhere and all places and wraps itself around you like so, a long embrace.

EPISODE 9

The Indiana Dunes National Lakeshore looms over Lake Michigan on its southern border and contains 15,000 acres of golden-hued, biologically diverse habitats. The dunes rise dramatically from the lake's shore—climbing 200 feet from the beaches and form valleys, ridges, and blowouts. In the seams between the dunes, wetlands flourish—packed with predacious bog plants that give way to prairie grasses and then tall white pines. Dunes by definition move at the command of wind and water; in this ecosystem, the enormous Mount Baldy, 126 feet in height, steps back away from the lake and into the nearby forest at a rate of four feet a year. Every time I visit these dunes, there is a new view. No one sees the same dune twice.

September: On Dunes

Mike arrived at the class barbecue uncharacteristically late. He found me out back, at the grill, sipping lemonade and shooing my children away from the spatter of hot dogs cooking over coals. It was a warm May afternoon and we were celebrating the end of school in the backyard on Dearborn Street in Iowa City. A picket fence framed the backyard and hot-pink roses were coming into bloom, rising on the trellis that framed the door. About fifteen students lounged around the yard, a pile on the hammock, clustered at the picnic table, looping arms around each other. This class had grown particularly close, through sharing personal essays over the entire school year, two semesters, thirty-two weeks, two hours per week, Tuesdays and Thursday mornings from ten until eleven in the morning. We were an ecosystem of personal stories. Like all ecosystems, we had our rules: No talking outside of class about the personal details revealed in class—that is, what happened in class, stayed in class. And no skipping class parties.

I can't stay, Mike said, placing a hand on his gut and making a face. All of his classmates within earshot wailed in protest.

Mike had been a late addition to the fall class, adding my section on the last day of drop-add, then shyly coming to my office hours after class to explain how he wanted to be a better writer and how he was not a great student in general and he wanted to change that. Then he sat there, looking at the snapshots taped to the wall above my desk, an uncurated collage of my children; friends from faraway; shrines and bridges—golden Buddha glistening in the sun and tall steel shrouded in rain; and many, many landscapes—the red rocks of Zion, the ice walls of Antarctica, the wild coasts of Maine. Among these the golden dunes of the Indiana Dunes National Park caught his eye.

Mike lit up. *Those are my dunes!* he said. *Good,* I said, *then you can write about them.* I explained how the golden dunes had dazzled me during the previous summer, an unexpected delight on a road trip from Iowa to Ohio to whiz around on roller coasters at Cedar Point with my children. My son had decided they were *Star Wars* dunes. Mike had grown up outside of Chicago and these sands were the stuff of his childhood. Yes, he said, *Star Wars* dunes.

He talked animatedly about their behavior, how they alternately sheltered and smothered trees, wetlands, and prairie grasses.

We agreed it was a capricious landscape indeed, a sharp contrast with the grotty stretch of rust belt towns hugging Lake Michigan. We also agreed the view from the summit—a view over another freakishly huge iteration on a familiar landscape feature—Lake Michigan, more inland sea than lake—was one of life's purest delights.

The next week, Mike came to my office to talk about the dunes and to drop off a book about the dunes. He also wanted advice about how to improve his flagging grade point average, how to see beyond his days of fraternity parties packed with friends, how to make the work-study job writing copy for events into a career in marketing, and he was hungry for good books for aspiring writers to read. He worried he was innately lazy and therefore would never succeed. I assigned him Virginia Woolf's *Street Haunting* and David Foster Wallace's *Consider the Lobster,* and the great scribe of landscapes and people, Loren Eiseley.

On that warm, bright afternoon in May, he handed me a bag of corn chips and a jar of cheese dip—I still wanted to bring some food by, so that I am here in spirit and then added, I really can't stay. I haven't been feeling so well. He also wanted to return *The Immense Journey* by Eiseley, borrowed from my library for inspiration for an essay about the Indiana Dunes Lakeshore. I told him to keep it and to give it back when he had a complete draft.

Someone called out, You're just hungover! You'll feel better if you eat a dog and have a brew. The atmosphere was animated and lively, people with no sense of time, the days entirely their own. If I didn't kick them out at sunset they would stay all night, talking and eating.

He shook his head. I stopped drinking a while ago, he said, in order to beat this bug.

Stay, they implored. They had made a sign and were all writing their names with glitter pens, haphazard calligraphy, hearts, words of love for one another. Mike said, I'll sign it next week, tiredly waving back to us as he turned and unlatched the white picket gate, I have to get going. I have some sort of bug I can't shake.

Two days later, I get a call from Gabe, another classmate. Mike had been in and out of the Student Health Services clinic for weeks. Finally, he had moved to the main hospital for further exams: They found cancer in his colon. After I hear this, I retreat to my Steelcase desk. Pull open the large, lower right drawer, stacked with papers and books. The shades on the windows the color of old parchment paper. The birds sing in the crabapple tree, whose riot of rosy flowers had so recently been like so many pink hands touching, and my neighbor tinkers with his riding lawnmower. I take a single aspirin in anticipation of the headache to come. The drawer contains information about the Indiana Dunes. And so I read.

Steep Sand Dunes and Magnificent Lake Views
Experience these sights at Indiana Dunes National Lakeshore
Waves crashing on sandy beaches
Karner blue butterflies landing on wild lupines
Peaceful silence lingering along winter trails
Bank swallows flying from their nests inside the dune

Henry Cowles was a University of Chicago field botanist and professor, ecologist, and conservationist who explored and described the dunes along Lake Michigan. He decoded the intricate ecosystem and recorded his findings in *The Ecological Relations of the Vegetation of the Sand Dunes of Lake Michigan* in 1899. This writing established him as the father of plant ecology in North America, and the Indiana dunes ecosystem became an international discussion. Yet in Indiana, the dunes were a prized resource fueling burgeoning industries.

True then and now: Scientists can only do so much to help redirect our capitalist gaze. How many of these stories do we need to write or hear about intricacy and beauty and complex life systems hammered into invisibility after being reclaimed as a natural resource for profit? *How many more stories.*

By the early twentieth century, industrial development crouched along the edge Lake Michigan and the sand dunes were their fuel. Those now-stylish canning jars made by the Ball Brothers, again closely associated with homey, organic pursuits? Ball glass fruit jars consumed much of a dune called Hoosier Slide, a 200-foot beauty. The rest headed off in railroad boxcars to Kokomo to become plate glass.

Cowles (pronounced Coals) watched Hoosier Slide carted off the face of the Earth with what I imagine was a singular rage. In 1908, he and others formed The Prairie Club of Chicago, and they proposed commercial interests be barred from carting off dunes along some portions of the lakefront. They used the words, "For the enjoyment of the people." The Dunes National Park Association also formed: "A national park for the Middle West, and all the Middle West for a national park."

A month after the National Park Service was created in 1916, the new agency's head, Stephen Mather, came to Chicago to gauge exactly how much fight people had in them to preserve the dunes—a spirit many hoped would lead to a Sand Dunes National Park. Hundreds attended the meeting, and Cowles was one of forty-two who spoke of the dunes. (The dunes gained national park status fifty years later, during the spike in the "back to nature" movement of the 1960s—wilderness preservation, clean water and lands, and open space for recreation.)

Cowles published very little after 1901, devoting himself instead to mentoring students, to field research, and his teaching. Perhaps Cowles envisioned education mimicking his ideas of plant succession, ideas traveling like so many seeds into the minds of his students, who then dispersed to new locales, taking the ideas with them.

Cowles' students are a dreamteam of twentieth-century ecology and land preservation advocates, Victor E. Shelford, father of animal ecology; George D. Fuller, who succeeded Cowles at Chicago; William Skinner Cooper, who refined the theories of plant succession; Paul B. Sears, who became professor of conservation at Yale and an essayist on all things ecological; and Walter P. Cottam, who founded the Nature Conservancy.

By the time the dunes gained national park status in 1966, many of the white pines had been logged. The farmers had arrived first, draining bogs and planting crops; they had been followed by heavy industry in East Chicago and Gary, Indiana. There was a housing boom in the 1930s, and this development accelerated in the post-war economic boom. Then a coal-fired power plant and steel mill were built in the midst of the wetlands and the dunes. Thus the dunes became a project for the National Park Service, restoring and reclaiming an ecosystem Cowles patrolled fifty years earlier.

In June, I received a note from Crystal, another classmate: *Mike is really sick. His parents moved him to Northwestern University Hospital in Chicago. I wanted to make sure you knew.*

Because my students wrote personal essays, I knew these students' lives, their work and aspirations, their youthful hopes and challenges. I can still clearly recall many of their essays, reading how Crystal paid her tuition by working as a bartender at the topless bar Dolls in Coralville, the next town over from Iowa City, a place for doughy, grabby men, who seemed to contain not an ounce of happiness. I read how Deana worked the factory line, soldering electronic components, a job that paid for a teaching degree at age 25. I read how Gabe worked in South Africa on community AIDS education.

One of my more experienced colleagues used to say there were two main types of students at Iowa: the kids from Iowa who knew more than they thought they did and had a sort of sweet curiosity, and the kids from Chicago who knew less than they thought they did and had come to Iowa as a safety school.

Most people don't get asked to narrate their lives in such detail or if they do, they don't necessarily get the full attention of the listener. It's not a complaint, just a statement of simple fact. It was because of this, because we were ready to see and hear each other—we formed the solid core unique to shared storytelling.

We were also tight because we were together the morning of September 11, 2001. The University of Iowa, like many schools, did not cancel classes after the attacks in New York, Washington, and Pennsylvania. So we writers met as we always did on the third floor of a Brutalist building on the banks of the Iowa River at 10 a.m. Central time. This meant we were all about 180 minutes into that hellish day.

We sat in the class for about ten minutes, crying or staring out the large windows or both, unable to look at text.

Then I said, *Let's all go home or somewhere and find the people we love. No one needs to be here. Everyone needs to be at home, watching television or listening to the radio. Or sitting quietly outside, taking in the day and letting this all sink in.*

As we gathered our things, Mike walked out with me. He felt bad that I had a bag heavy with graded assignments I had neglected to give out and insisted on carrying it for me.

I have nothing else to do but watch TV. They will all be watching TV at my fraternity, and I don't want to watch TV now, he said.

He walked me halfway home, to College Green Park, toting the sack.

While we walked, he talked about the writing we were supposed to critique that day. He was envious of Deana's writing, among the best in the class in his opinion. We had just read about her life as a solderer at the Motorola plant, which showed her both working the line and also sitting, exhausted, in front of her assigned locker, before heading home to take care of her nine-year-old daughter. She had her daughter when she was 16. At the factory, she came to know women who had been soldering for many years. The essay was also a narrative of color photos of cats carefully taped on the inside of lockers and how the women talked about their cats waiting for them at home, what they ate, what sorts of attitudes they had. It was those cats that made her desperate to get free, so she scraped to save money, to attend college at 25, to become a second-grade teacher.

He wanted to talk about how she did it. I asked him to answer his own question. *How did she do it?* Mike said it was the voice and the voice was all these details. Like the peeling tape inside those metal lockers. Like how some of the cats in the pictures in the lockers were deceased and the women mourned each other's pets. How they talked more about cats than themselves or the world.

The other essay we had read was by a writer from western Iowa, where family farms collapsed and towns were decimated by meth and Walmart and corporate mega farms. This one covered losing the family farm to a corporate predator, then the family moving into a town where both parents took jobs that made them unrecognizable to the writer—the mother as a bank teller and the father as an insurance salesperson, no longer the farm family, running combines, putting food by from their prodigious garden, watching a million lightning bugs explode in the June night sky.

All that I have, he said forlornly, is a story of leaving a happy home to come to college at Iowa.

That Motorola essay threw me off, he said, glancing at the sky. I can't write like that.

Why not, I asked. You've got such a great knack for story.

As he walked away, he said, I can't write like that because nothing bad has ever happened to me.

Later that term, Mike turned in an essay about how he came back to sit in College Green Park in the days after 9/11 and thought about how he was living too slow. He wrote through a quiet moment, sitting there watching the light patchwork in old trees, watching young families and wondering what sort of father he'd be—because he couldn't quite imagine being a father and yet he felt that soon he'd be married, with a steady job, and a baby to take to the park. It was a gorgeous little essay by a writer trying to get across a closely held feeling and point and as I read it, I understood that it must have hatched in his brain as we talked about those cat photos.

I wondered whom to contact for more information about Mike. Other students? No. That was a rabbit hole of misinformation and hysteria. My journalist instincts kicked in. I had to find his family. Then I recalled Mike had an uncle by marriage in town, a filmmaker well known for a documentary about the legendary Iowa wrestler Dan Gable.

I went through the Iowa City phone book and found his name, then tentatively punched in the number. On the machine I explained how I was Mike's teacher and wanted to get any news I could.

He called me back in the morning.

Mike had been feeling sick for some time, he said, and went to Student Health Services over a few months, trying to figure out what was wrong.

When I heard this, I wondered why Mike had never mentioned his stomach to me. I would have kicked into mother-gear, I told the uncle. I would have told him to forget that student service and go to the big hospital on the hill where they had real doctors. I felt the rage rising in me. Student health gave him medication for a sour stomach, but the pain didn't abate. They saw him repeatedly. Finally, he was sent to the university hospital for a more granular look. By the time Mike was evaluated there, cancer had gone wild in his gut.

Summer was upon us in Iowa, it was a steam bath; temperatures hit the high 80s, humidity twinning along. The updates continued from students and the uncle: Mike started chemotherapy. They decided not to operate and stick with chemotherapy. All moved along.

Students called me, upset. I reassured them: Picture Mike in my office in a couple months. I will have you all over for a dinner. We will all stay together in this.

I imagined those meetings, with me saying, When you were in the hospital all I could think about was the time you said you had nothing to write about. Well, you sure challenged the gods, didn't you? Now you have material that is going to own that writing room. I pictured us laughing about this in my basement office in the English-Philosophy Building.

I pictured him saying, I think I'll write about something else, other than my illness. Instead, maybe he'd write about his beloved dunes, the Indiana Dunes National Lakeshore as I had asked him to on many occasions. Then we would go back to our weekly meetings and he would graduate and send me Christmas cards for the rest of my life. The cards would have photos—of a wife, a baby, then two babies, and he would work in Chicago in public relations for some sports team, which was a dream of his, and go to baseball games with his kids.

These dialogues with the imagined Mike were fueled by sporadic emails from the man himself. I heard from Mike three times that summer, always in response to notes from me. The picture of Mike in my head: Sitting in a hospital bed, getting chemotherapy, getting better, laptop nearby, enjoying cheery notes from me and the class about what he could write about when he got back to Iowa City, where he was so badly missed.

I wrote longish notes on banal topics—weather, student drunken-driving arrests in Iowa City, the new Japanese restaurant, how my daughter was doing in swim lessons, how our mutual friend Gabe seemed to be doing. We called Gabe the Mayor of Iowa City, because everywhere we went with him, he knew ninety percent of the people.

Mike's brief words that summer offered but one sentiment: Thanks for all your support. It did not sound like him. But then again, I had never engaged in email conversations with Mike: Maybe there was a disconnect from the in-person to the email correspondent? Maybe chemo was harder than the uncle made it out to be?

It didn't occur to me at the time that it was not Mike who was responding. This thought only came to me much later.

The idea of nature as a weave of interdependent systems goes back to the ancient Greeks. Charles Darwin reignited the discussion by making it impossible to think of life separated from environment, arguing that environment had built itself into the organization and the very form of life.

Indiana Dunes National Lakeshore is fifteen miles of beach seemingly squashed into a landscape choked by industrial sprawl. It's peculiar how industrial squalor can do this to the natural world, make it look out of place.

The national park is comprised of four major dune complexes, the youngest dunes forming sinuous ridges near the lake. The size of a sand dune here can vary from a couple inches to several stories high. Each dune is unique, its own entity, formed from glacial drift, pushed by wind. The older dune lines are named Tolleston, Calumet, and Glenwood. The latter two formations press into a stable oak forest, creating what is called a ghost forest.

Nearby Gary, Indiana, is a cluttered mess of built environment long past its prime. The dunes themselves offer a mirroring effect of these failed human systems in their ghost forests. Tall oaks and other trees overtaken by the marching sands. The trees in the older dunes slowly succumb to the sand, overcome, strangled by the shifting sands. As they die, their silvery trunks extend from golden sand, so many arrows hurled towards Earth's surface from an unseen and relentless god. The ghost forest gives the dunes a creepy feel, a sharp contrast from all the species seen and felt, crammed into the space, making a hopeful stand and recovery.

When I started to research the dunes, how curious to find Cowles's field notes, letters, and manuscripts were gone: After he died, all of his writings vanished, destroyed or discarded by family members. His daughter Harriet, noted as having played a role in this, apparently felt nobody would be interested in his work and thus found little reason to save any of his writing.

Students thread back into Iowa City in early August and classes loom mid-month. Gabe was the first to arrive at my house, showing up sweaty and smiling on his bike. Gabe who had spent his junior year in Africa, teaching HIV prevention techniques, Gabe the buoyant and hopeful.

Gabe offered the news Mike would soon arrive. He was still undergoing treatment but Mike wanted to be back in his beloved college town, with his fraternity brothers.

Over the next two weeks, I heard diverse and contradictory stories from students. In one, Mike had rented an apartment. In another he was moving back into the fraternity. In another he was coming back but not taking classes. In another he was not coming back. His uncle reported in periodic phone calls the family remained optimistic but gave no specific details.

That August in Iowa the heat hung down and compressed the town, indeed the whole state. Old folks were found dead in un-air conditioned trailers, and chickens reportedly exploded from heat in hen houses. I had three old wall air conditioners, one in my study, one in the dining room, and one upstairs. My children, then seven and three, walked around in cotton underpants, running out the kitchen door, into the back yard, where they sprayed each other with the green hose, and then back into the dining room, where they stood on the wood floor dripping in front of the sputtering wall unit, condenser wheezing.

It was on just such a day I got the call. I sat at my green Steelcase desk, bought at the university surplus center for forty-five dollars, the backs of my shorts-clad legs painfully adhering to an blue-vinyl desk chair. My son sprinted into the room, phone in wet hand and said, It's for you.

Mike's uncle was on the phone.

Mike died yesterday, he said. I stared at the picket fence outside my window, the same gate he had last walked through, complaining of a bad stomach. The last time I saw him.

Mike never got off the mats, he said, a reference to wrestling, a situation where an opponent takes you down and you cannot get up. He told me how the chemo or some other drug had made Mike's legs enormous, so big he could not stand or really comfortably sit. He had not wanted people to see his legs. Then they could not get on top of the cancer, and he died. I had never met the uncle, did not know what he looked like, and I was trying to picture what sort of expression was on his face when he delivered that last, sad bit of information.

I said OK in what sounded like a weird, hollow version of my voice and then asked him to stay in touch. Then I said I could not talk and I dropped the phone and ran into the bathroom and threw up.

I stretched out on the cool tile and tried to recall why I had not taken the time in June or July to drive the four hours to Chicago and see him at the hospital.

I did not attend Mike's funeral, although I told his family that I would. The day before the funeral, I loaded my children in the car and headed for Chicago but decided about 100 miles into the drive that instead we would go to the sand dunes. When we passed the place where I should have turned off of the interstate and headed north to the Chicago suburb where he would be buried, I gripped the steering wheel and looked ahead.

Before I left, one of his fraternity brothers had called and said, we'll see you at the funeral. We had met at Mike's twenty-first birthday in a bar. I never went to twenty-first birthday parties, but Gabe and the rest of the class had talked me into it.

The friend on the phone said, I thought you would like to know how much you meant to Mike. He never had met a teacher he could talk to before you, and talking to you made him want to make better grades.

The fellow paused. I also thought you'd like to have the photo of you guys he had? Unless you have a copy? I told him to drop the photo off in my box in the English-Philosophy Building.

Blowouts, shaped like amphitheaters, are places where the wind has carved away the dunes, exposing stands of long-dead trees. Some call them tree cemeteries. Some talk about them as being akin to the rise and fall of great empires. Whirling, pushing winds challenge stands of plants. It was in the Indiana dunes that Cowles developed his concept of plant succession, earning for the dunes the nickname, Birthplace of Ecology.

Here's how a blowout operates in fact: As the wind breaks barrier plant life away, it is free to push through the sand, creating a straight path back to stands of trees. In the dunes, you can find stands of cottonwoods, now so many decaying trunks, trees that helped create the dunes in the first place, far-reaching roots holding the shifting sands in place. They could seize and hold the earth. Their leaves fell to the ground where they offered, in decay, life to other plants. As the trees held their ground, piling sand slowly began to bury them. They died before the sand reached their highest branches. The dead trees no longer help the earth in place, the wind savagely pushed through, digging out a blowout in the dune. But in this act of annihilation, plant succession began. A new generation of so-called pioneer plants came in and established communities.

When you stand in their midst, blowouts create a dramatic view of Lake Michigan—a wide, steep, deep, canyon-view of the water. Crouching in a blowout today, you can see what Cowles observed and named, marram grass, puccoon flowers, as well as young oaks and cottonwoods ready to fight another day, against sand and wind and time.

When I returned from the dunes, I pedaled my bike to my campus office. In my English-Philosophy Building box was an envelope. In the envelope was a photo of Gabe, me, and Mike. The note said, Mike kept this pinned up by his bed in the fraternity with a few other pictures of his family.

A year later, I received a Fulbright to go to New Zealand with my family to write a book about Antarctica. The students of the nonfiction writing class of 2001–02 had graduated and scattered back to Chicago, Des Moines, some went to graduate school in law, joined the Army, some stayed put.

Gabe moved to Beijing, and we stayed in touch by email. As I packed up the house, I scanned the photo and sent it to Gabe.

I found his reply in my inbox a few days later.

I still think about Mike a lot. I never think about him as dead, I just think about him the person, he was so alive, and still is, I guess. Where he still lives on in the way I remember him, my memory, that part is as alive as it ever will be. The death part never makes sense, and it never will as far as I am concerned. The question of why is somewhat inapplicable, and the lack of understanding is the only norm I think can exist.

I gaze at us smiling, arms looped around one another, and remember the dark, upstairs bar not seen in the photo, packed with students and sticky tables and blaringly loud with rock music. I also think about standing on those dunes, and how the dunes are moved by wind, how the wind and sand work on the white pine forest. Dunes by their very definition are loose sand moved by external elements—air or water. I think how the dunes were saved from miners who wanted to freeze them into glass containers and how there is a strange beauty in the trees' entombment in the sand and how when you walk through the trees to the summit line, the water of the great lake called Michigan awaits, spilling over the edge of the world.

NOTEBOOK NINE

*An aerial view of San Francisco. A city with swathes of open space.
The northern nib being the Presidio, the large rectangle stretching
west to the Pacific Ocean being Golden Gate Park. Between
Golden Gate Park and the Presidio are neighborhoods called The
Richmond, Sea Cliff, Presidio Terrace. The Richmond covers what
were once vast seas of golden sand dunes, once a place for dairy
cows and orphanages, Playland, and the Sutro Baths.*

I walk from my home to a small garden shop in The Richmond,
in search of cabbage seedlings for my Presidio Community
Garden. I walk down Battery Caulfield Road and cross out of
the national park. The Richmond is an aesthetically erratic and
often ugly neighborhood, Edwardians squished together in a
bizarre hodgepodge with apartment buildings from the 1970s.

Ropes of insane electrical wires festoon its streets. What sort of
code do they comply with, I ponder, the madman-public utilities
code? Loops are tethered on one end to a tilted utility pole and
on the other to a nest of wires cutting into a home or homes.
They create a wild tangle of wires that frame and deconstruct
the continuity of the grey sky in a postmodern way. The garden
shop is tucked into a side street near a Korean barbecue place and
a pizza parlor. Tall silver racks of tiny plants line the sidewalk,
heirloom tomatoes, pole beans, lemon cucumbers, thyme, purple
basil, mint, Japanese eggplants. My garden is rather small, about
four feet by eight feet. Yet I have land baron aspirations when it
comes to planting herbs and vegetables. I want them all.

I settle for a small flat of six silvery, hopeful cabbage plants.
Inside, as I fish around for my money, a tall display of terrariums
invites further study. They range in size from tiny glistening
vessels holding a single pale succulent, to twenty-gallon jugs
offering tangled worlds of orchids, succulents, and mosses.

I had not thought a terrarium could be such a compelling
object. The terrariums of my youth were made in Camp Fire

girl craft sessions and were as much about layers of gaudy bright-colored sand as about what we grew in them. We Camp Fire girls wore red and blue polyester jumpers, white blouses, and blue hats. While some in our ranks found this outfit repellent, I adored the get-up and the craft-making it signaled. I recall pouring in layers of pink, yellow, and orange sand, adding a wafer-thin layer of black here and there for delineation. I recall how we used mainly philodendron and a plant the troop leader called Wandering Jew.

The fact our troop never got near an actual campfire, never hiked, nor jumped into ponds as the girls on the brochures did was not discussed.

I pondered the micro-eco systems encased in glass. How delicate the condensation. The long, determined reach of an orchid with an impossibly tiny orange flower, all gathered into an artful statement of a human hand and brain engaging glass and plant. Glass and plants make such companionable partners.

While I lingered, gazing at pale green succulents nestled in sandy foundations, I recalled a book about how environments choose the plants and animals that inhabit them.

Even the people. One example offered: cliff dwellings in the American Southwest. Inhabitants apparently left because of climate change, the rock and sand studied, photographed, continuing to dazzle human eyes, a story of place shape-shifted by people no longer part of the story. The argument, as I recall, was that sand and rock beckoned people in to make something grand, something sand and rock could not do on their own. How did I feel about all of this? Impossible to know. On one hand I would like to be someone who could and would believe. On the other hand. Well, the other hand is actually two hands, the hands writing this book that you are now reading. These hands want to consider how we get our hands on places, design and otherwise alter them, and what it means when we draw them. These hands are connected to a brain of two minds about the ability of soil to make us do its bidding. Although there's something in this that is deeply satisfying—as we are all in conversation with materials. But maybe from a more neutral standpoint we can say that gardening, or building cliff dwellings in the desert, is all of the same instinct. The instinct called to go forth and change the way things work on the Earth's surface. Maybe we are hard-wired for modification. Perhaps leaving things the way they are is simply not part of being human.

The beginning of human settlement in the Presidio, besides soldiers and Native Americans, sprung up around El Polin Spring. The Presidio as an assignment or an escape or a refuge—immigrant people who wound up here in the early days were either sent by the military or wandered in, escaping some other place.

A local stone carver was commissioned in 2005 to add Woodrow Wilson's words to the Immigrant Point overlook: The quote reads: "We opened the gates to all the world and said: 'Let all men who want to be free come to us and they will be welcome.'"

EPISODE 10

According to the Greeks, trees are an alphabet. —Roland Barthes

October: On Forest as Text

There were no environmental activists where I am from. People didn't do that sort of thing. There were some people who had protested the Vietnam War by selling POW/MIA bracelets that were silver cuffs stamped with a man's name, rank, and the date he was lost or taken captive. I was not allowed to own one. Neither of my parents seemed to notice that I ordered publications of an environmental watchdog nature, or if they did, they did not comment. There was a group called Earthwatch and you could work for them, doing things like counting songbirds in cities and tracking the effects of light pollution on what times they awoke and sang. I read about this work and imagined myself doing something similar, recording the lives of the birds. While I look out at the trees many days and write fervently, I do not write of the lives of birds. No, it has been my path to follow the lives of trees. There is something hidden in the fabric of the forest. I saw an understanding of that inclination or notion in the work of the ecologists, arborists, and botanists, the nature writers and the artists whose work has caught my eye.

I put on my boots and walked out the front door towards the stand of trees formerly on the corner of Washington and Lincoln. They were no more. It is deeply sad when trees are felled and even the tree choppers felt this, or so I surmised. I had my camera and was taking photos of the chopped-down trees, and one of the forestry crew drove up and wanted to know why I was taking pictures. He told me people had been taking photos and writing articles and complaining about cutting down trees and those people did not understand forestry. I did not have an answer. I just shrugged and walked home and sat with my precious books, whose pages were made of trees.

Some days in the Presidio after the walks and before it is time to drive the car to take children to baseball games or pick them up from practices, there's nothing left to do but sit at my desk and cast my eyes around the bookshelves in my studio. I have a lot of books about trees, forests, and art about trees and forests. There are histories of people writing about nature, dating to the ancient Greeks. There are polemics, arguing for nature, by Thoreau and other Americans. There are scientists offering research about how whole ecosystems are thrown out of whack by climate chaos and what that means for trees.

My collection is a far cry from a library and the precious books, and I like it that way. The books are organized in a particular manner, by topic and also by where they were purchased, such as at the DK Bookstore in Bangkok, at Prairie Lights in Iowa City, at Kramerbooks & Afterwords in Washington, DC. Some live together from my childhood—replacements, the originals all pitched out by my mother during one of my parents' many house moves—*Pickles The Fire Cat, Where the Wild Things Are, The Lonely Doll,* and *The Little House* by Virginia Lee Burton. This last one is the story of a house at first cheerfully located in the countryside and then claustrophobically trapped by a city that grows and surrounds her over many days and years.

As much as I like reading the books, I like to find out who the writers are—how did they wind up writing, what were they mining in their writing, where had they lived, what had they thought about when not writing, how they fared in life. This is also part of the collection—I know a little about all of the writers. None of the writers are complete strangers to me. I read up on Burton, who won the Caldecott Medal for the book—the highest prize for illustrated children's books—and learned Burton's writing and artwork were deliberately constructed to reflect concerns that industrialization was destroying aesthetic elements she deemed essential. The book arcs across decades, as the city slowly emerges and then overwhelms the little house.

The passage of time is depicted by the rising and setting of many suns and moons. When she accepted the Caldecott, Burton said that she had decided a child could understand the passage of time through "the waxing and waning of the moon, the succession of the days of the month; and the rotations of the seasons, the evanescence of the year."

The Little House also resonated for the young me in Maryland. It was less fiction, more news report. I lived that experience: Fields once packed with an array of butterflies, the cabbage white, eastern swallowtail, and giant swallowtails; cattails lining ponds, snapping turtles sunning themselves on the rocks, the occasional waxy-white dogwood jumbled in with a mess of elms and pines. In their place, olive-drab aluminum-sided houses, one-story schools of pale brick, lines of empty and newly occupied shops—Hairport beauty salon; Auf Wiedersehen, a German restaurant always empty; Hallmark card store where they sold Little Charmers figurines; all hunkered down beside empty parking lots. Summer lost the scent of honeysuckle and humid woods, replaced by hot macadam and tar flattened by steamrollers as new roads then filled with cars. Burton's *Little House:* The house is soon hidden by multistory buildings and an elevated highway. The house is then found and saved—moved back to a hillside in the country, surrounded by trees covered with pink blossoms, a child swings from the tree swing, a man mows the lawn with a push mower, robins fly in the sky: Once again she was lived in and taken care of.

In a biography of Burton by Barbara Elleman, the author notes that *The Little House* reflected a pastoral theme common to American literature and that Burton was once asked if the point of *The Little House* was that the further away we get from nature and the simple way of life, the less happy we are. Burton said she was, "quite willing to let this be its message."

The DC suburbs: No one was from there. Everyone from Pennsylvania or New York or South Carolina or Germany or Iran or Korea. It was like we had all fallen from some basket tipped over in the sky, scattered into the new homes that sprang from the red clay into look-alike burgs, Norbeck Meadows, Flower Valley, Mill Creek Towne, sets of model homes, three or four floor plans in each, referred to as a development or a subdivision or an area. No one used the word town. Maybe no one could because no one knew what the place was or how we all wound up there.

Facing out from a shelf is the photo book of Frederic Edwin Church's home, Olana, in the Hudson River Valley, a large villa that sits on a high hill and overlooks the river as it winds down towards the sea. Church designed it after he returned from travels in the Middle East. Architectural historians emphasized that it was a hard place to categorize in terms of the aesthetic. Persian? Maybe.

I had made the pilgrimage there with Jennifer, a friend for decades, since we were colleagues at *The Washington Post* when we were just out of college, back when we were both planning other lives outside the confines of Washington, DC. I was going to report the news in exotic locales, and Jennifer was going to become a psychoanalyst. Every once in a while when we feel buried under our respective caravans, children, car repairs, weird men, we remind each other that those young versions of us would be pleased with most of what had transpired, one or two poor choices of husband aside. And we are here to tell the story, Jennifer would add in her gorgeous laugh.

Olana is unique in that most home/villa combinations from the great, historic American artists are no longer extant. Jennifer parked her navy Volvo station wagon in a gravelly lot, and we walked the short winding path towards the villa. We had bought our tickets, during fall colors, long in advance. A small group waited at the entrance, a massive door. A group of disappointed Swiss tourists who lacked tickets stood by forlornly. One the men kept repeating in a harsh yet disappointed tone, *But I do not understand what the procedure is. What is the procedure for entry?*

A door was pulled open by a tiny elderly woman with a neat grey bob and pearls. She ushered us in, then offered a seamless narration of the home and Church's life as we paused in the rooms, which we learned are almost entirely, precisely the way they were when Church worked and lived in them. Brushes haphazardly leading out of cups, large easels, gorgeous sombreros from his many trips to Mexico, where he wintered.

Church's work vividly documents wild nature. He was inspired by the explorer Alexander von Humboldt—who wrote up descriptions of both his explorations and his thoughts in a series of best-selling books and who vigorously encouraged artists to come along on his explorations, to sketch and paint and show the wild world in all its dense glories. In this, Humboldt was a catalyst in getting Church deep into the Amazon. The Amazon in the nineteenth century. I stood in Olana's dim rooms and wondered about the man who would travel to such a place in those times: There were so many things that could take a person out in the nineteenth-century Amazon. And yet Church went, called by the idea artists brought a place to clear view for the rest of us. That the world deserved to see all the beauty of fierce nature. We climbed a wide staircase to a room—a bedroom converted into an exhibition space—where a tiny show was laid out. It displayed Humboldt's massive treatises on the flora and fauna of the Amazon—and explored precisely how these words beckoned Church to paint the Amazon and how it fueled the larger public imagination.

Back in Manhattan the next day, I took the subway to The Metropolitan Museum of Art to see *Heart of the Andes* in person. The work astonished me as it had the world when it was revealed. The painting was shown in New York City in 1859 at the Lyrique Hall, and more than 12,000 people paid twenty-five cents (equivalent to eight dollars today but also a time when a pair of work boots cost two dollars). The painting is 67 inches by 120 inches. In the twenty-first century world of LED signs screaming messages into our eyes in Times Square, it holds its own, projecting and amplifying a vivid sense of place. The painting holds the eye in a particular moment of fascination. I sat on a bench and stared at the painting and thought of the story of Olana. In the early 1950s, a Yale doctoral student named David Huntington was researching Church and his work at Olana. It was not a crowded area of inquiry: Church was largely forgotten by then. This had given me pause, the idea that in 1860 he was building this estate and people were lining up in the thousands to see his work and then, boom, gone and forgotten. Except by this one art historian who gets hooked on the Hudson River School and winds up at Olana, which turned out to be largely undisturbed, the attic packed with hundreds of Church's landscape sketches and paintings. I get too close to the painting, and the guard hurries over to tell me to back off. That's OK, I got what I wanted, an intimate second of seeing those intricate strokes of detail. Church's eye and hand at work. Marvelous.

On the lowest shelf, within easy grasp if I lean at a precarious angle, there's a series of palm-sized art history books, covers the color of fresh milk. I reach for the volume on John Constable, cover gently peeling, printed in Holland in 1963. Designed by Wim van Stek and Aart Verhoeven. I acquired a lot of the art books at an auction in San Francisco, the same one where I acquired my moon-gazing chair and Thai Buddhist document cabinet in the late 1980s. These small books were stuffed in one of the boxes, quite a surprise. Barnes & Noble published the Art Series—back when it had a store at 705 Fifth Avenue and the Constable book "is one of a series presenting selected works of the masters. Each contains more than fifty illustrations of the artist's work: twenty-four of these high-quality color reproductions. The text, by recognized experts, gives a concise survey of the life and work of each artist with brief comments on the influences which inspired him."

When I first encountered Constable's work, I was perhaps ten. Our class made an annual trek to the National Gallery of Art in

Washington, DC, piling into an orange bus for the bouncing ride across DC's still riot-wrecked streets, the rubes rolling into the city from Norbeck Meadows for an annual art inoculation.

Constable was born in 1776—the same year Europeans took hold of the Presidio and also the year the current environmental redesign is pegged for establishing what, precisely is "native" to the Presidio. Constable often painted his native Suffolk, once writing how the Suffolk countryside inspired his painting, "the sound of water escaping from mill dams etc., willows, old rotten planks, slimy posts, and brickwork, I love such things." Constable also wrote, "Painting is but another word for feeling."

The author of this small book is Phoebe Pool; the Constable book, Pool's second, following *Picasso, The Formative Years: A Study of His Sources*. I searched for Pool's name across the web and found her in a 2005 obituary for Jenifer Hart, Oxford don and public intellectual. Hart died at age 91 and had been a contemporary of Pool's at Oxford. Pool was born in the midst of the Great War and admitted to Somerville College, Oxford, in 1931 to study history on a scholarship but left without graduating. Pool later completed a PhD at the University of London under the mentorship of Anthony Blunt. I looked back at the little beige Constable book—Blunt was listed as its co-author, too. She wrote for *The Spectator*, taught at the University of Reading, and did research at The Courtauld Institute of Art, where she was a fixture. One biography described her writing as simple but not simplistic. This turn of phrase gave me pause. Simple but not simplistic. The accounting of Hart's life—a long and storied life, included this: "In his book *Spycatcher* (1987), however, (Peter) Wright revealed that Jenifer Hart had been identified as a member of the "Oxford Ring," a covert Communist cell, by fellow member Phoebe Pool, who had been named by the Soviet spy and art historian Anthony Blunt as his courier during the 1930s. Both Phoebe Pool and her fellow cell member, the Labour MP Bernard Floud, committed suicide in 1967 shortly after MI5 had interrogated Floud about his KGB connections."

I read the Constable monograph in the hot, white light of sunset on the western edge of the Presidio with a fresh sense of intrigue—the art historians all spies. Betrayal. Suicide. Deceit. My little art books felt more edgy. Pool writes, Constable's influence on the Barbizon School cannot be overstated. I wondered about the ecosystem of British Communist Party activities and imagined a world of art historians in the 1930s in Oxford and London feeling it was incumbent upon them to join up and work towards a greater socialist world order. I wonder how disappointed they must have felt when Stalin's atrocities were laid bare. I wonder if the Courtauld collection gave Pool solace and if the words *"Ars longa, vita brevis"* floated through her mind. I thought about how hard it is to be a person of your times in general and how odd it was that so many years later the hunt for communists would cast such a peculiar net that a research scholar and writer and an MP would feel compelled to take their own lives, when Hart and Blunt did not.

I take the book to the kitchen and put on the kettle for a cup of Earl Grey tea. Living in New Zealand completely shaped my tea habit. I cannot get through the day without a cup of milky tea at 4 p.m. or so. I look out my subterranean kitchen window, the front of the townhouse is rammed into the dunes, a split level design, and watch a boa of eucalyptus leaves rassle in the wind. They make a distinctive sound, these gum trees. The tall ones creak like an attic door opening in a horror film, the leaves sound like a baby's rattling toy. Constable wrote, I shall paint my own places best. I put the Constable book down on the counter and pour hot water into my orange tea pot. The smell of bergamot fills the kitchen. I imagine Pool sitting in the Courtauld archives—a place where I was told to turn down my music while doing research because others could hear it coming from the ear pieces (David Bowie)—writing with a small nib of pencil in a notebook about Constable for a book I never wrote. Picture her: In an olive tweed jacket and long brown wool skirt, hat pulled down, owlish glasses, walking home from the Courtauld as the afternoon light fades, across busy, dirty London streets, happy to be near completion of the Constable book, a book she desperately needed to complete because she needed the money. As she sauntered along, trapezoids of citrusy light illuminate stone made over many thousands of years, monumental stone, and she allows herself to be lost in the immutability of art, and the quicksand of politics feels distant indeed.

I sip my tea and look out the window and spy so many fallen euc leaves burying my succulents in the outdoor planters, and this needs to be attended to. Time to don the gloves and root out the old leaves so the succulents can thrive. Roland Barthes writes there is a Greek saying that trees are an alphabet. If we agree an alphabet is a system and that a system is developed to respond, elastically, to challenges in an orderly way, and if we agree that trees and their representation in a painting are also a system for understanding what it means to walk in the forest: Then I agree.

The Presidio is a wet forest.

NOTEBOOK TEN

Walking on Baker Beach at 8:30 a.m. Three men film waves breaking on the beach. They have a huge, rounded grey microphone and stand where the surf breaks. I ask them what they are doing. And they tell me they are filming a documentary on wave energy for the local power utility company.

Daniel Burnham had a hand in the Presidio, he of the World's Columbarian Fair in Chicago and the Flatiron Building in New York, among others, and considered in those days perhaps America's preeminent architect. Burnham once famously said, "Make no little plans. They have no magic to stir men's blood and probably will not themselves be realized."

Between 1902 and 1906, Burnham visited San Francisco to assist the city in its "Improvement and Adornment." On at least one occasion, in 1904, he met with the commanding officer of the Presidio. A record of their conversation does not exist except that they discussed the "beautification" of the Presidio. Some of Burnham's recommendations:

• **Arranging the drives and concourses so that the public may enjoy the best views of the landscape**

• **Enlarging the present parade ground and locating the post headquarters on its main axis**

• **Creating a vast drill ground**

• **Creating a great terrace on the west to provide a view of the Golden Gate**

• **Enclosing the parade ground with terraces of slight elevation**

• **Burnham's work in the city was brought to a halt temporarily by the 1906 earthquake and fire. Burnham's hand is seen in Park Presidio Boulevard, which links the Presidio to Golden Gate Park.**

In the Presidio Archives, researching the architectural and landscape design, I come across Army Engineer Major William W. Harts, who came to California immediately following the

1906 earthquake. While I had seen much about Major William Albert Jones, the famed landscape designer of the Presidio, this was my first look at Harts. He graduated from West Point in 1889 and became a lieutenant in the Engineers, serving on harbor and river projects across the U.S. When he arrived in San Francisco, he had already served as a mine-layer in the Spanish-American War, where he was severely wounded.

During 1907, he developed plans to enlarge and beautify the Presidio and Fort Mason. It was Major Harts who lobbied the Army to drop its dreary architecture styles in the Presidio and embrace the Spanish Colonial/Mission Revival styles, which were popular in the local civilian community. Harts' *Report Upon the Expansion and Development of the Presidio of San Francisco,* is considered to be the first "comprehensive master plan" for the Presidio.

Harts noted the Presidio as a site of great beauty, "is probably excelled by no other military post in the world in the magnificence of its location and its commanding position."

He observed that a third of the Presidio had trees—eucalyptus, spruce, and pine, with ridges gently dividing the Presidio into three parts. At the time, the Presidio was imagined as a place where 310 officers, 9,833 enlisted men, 2,667 horses, 177 wagons, and 352 buildings would crowd in. This was never realized. On the *Map of the Presidio of San Francisco California* showing the proposed new arrangement of barracks, officers quarters, new building, roads, gardens, and forestation he draws in the built environment across the sinewy contour lines.

He states:

"It is well known . . . that the architecture of government buildings on military posts has in the past unfortunately always been of a needlessly plain character . . . The arrangement of barracks and quarters in the form of a hollow square . . . formerly adopted on level plains for self protection in the days of Indian troubles, has still been followed in cases where other plans would would have suited the site far better. The use of straight lines for roads . . . and long straight rows of buildings is still followed . . . partly from custom and partly from . . . indifferent to appearances. The standard double set of officers' quarters formerly built for economy in heating and to save a small amount of construction, is still used in spite of the protests of the officers who live in them."

EPISODE ELEVEN

November: On Brains

I t is Thanksgiving Day and I am walking on Mount Tamalpais. On Thanksgiving Day, 1921, the renowned botanist Alice Eastwood walked this terrain as she often did, footsteps even across the slipping soil and rocks, this mountain a preferred site for her work as the California Academy of Sciences lead botanist. Mount Tamalpais is a short drive from San Francisco, across the Golden Gate Bridge, then up winding mountain roads to trail heads, and with a backpack filled with orange notebook, shiny phone, vacuum bottle of tea, and a cheese sandwich, I am able to sustain a long walk through these woods. In Eastwood's day, crossing the Golden Gate meant a ferry ride across churning waters, followed by a cumbersome ride to the mountain. But it was an easy trip compared to her walks in the distant Sierra Nevadas, kneeling, bowing down, seeking plant species as though in prayer.

As I climb higher across the narrow trail, switchback a steep climb up on one side and a sharp drop on the other, I hear her words: This list was made on a Thanksgiving Day in a year when Mount Tamalpais was favored by early fall rains. These favorable weather conditions awakened some of the spring flowers from their dormant condition and kept many of the summer flowers still in bloom. San Francisco in those days—shortly before the turn of the century—was hills and dunes and scrub. It was the Wild West. The Barbary Coast. Hordes of sailors and miners, a wind-tossed, sandy thumb of scrub and bounteous wild flowers.

Mount Tam stands at 2,751 feet, and Eastwood's name is emblazoned on trail and campsite. This is how I came to know her because she did not appear in any of the books that had been used to teach me about science in any school. I paused on the trail and sipped some coffee. In fact, I could not recall learning anything about the American West except from television, from shows like *The Cisco Kid* and *Here Come the Brides* and movies like *True Grit*. The West was a place of drunks and horses and ladies and the occasional outlaw or Indian. I walked on. Eastwood was renowned among the scientists of her day, revered in the competitive world of botanizing for identifying and collecting seeds and plants across the Bay Area, Mount Tam, the Presidio, the Berkeley Hills, and then into the Sierras, cataloging seeds and other specimens, writing extensively about her classifications. On her 1921 walk, for instance, she identified more than 100 species on Mount Tam; vascular plants including ferns, horsetails, flowering plants, and conifers. When the weather cooperates, and the fall is wet, pops of brilliant color weave into the thick, woody ambiance, the bright purples of calypsa bulbosa fairy slipper and iris; the green bottle-brush forms of equisetem, horsetail, and the varigated, painterly lines of *scoliopus bigelovii,* California fetid Adder's tongue.

Eastwood's talent and ferocity for exploration and discovery are particularly compelling when you take into consideration the fact that she lived in times when the halls of science were almost entirely closed to her gender—and the fact that botanical classification was close to a blood sport in those days. How things were discovered, named, how new species were verified and who got credit, this woman who stepped into the fierce maelstrom of academic botany had a steel spine. She knew what she was taking on and she worked hard and she prevailed. Eastwood wrote more than 300 scientific papers and developed a seed collection nonpareil at the California Academy of Sciences, where she worked for more than four decades. I liked Alice Eastwood; on days when I was being a cry baby writer about some minor setback around the stringing together of words for publication or pay or both, I would stop and look at her photo, Alice resting on a trip in the Sierras. She was one badass botanist.

Born in Toronto in 1859, she and her family relocated to Denver in 1873. The highest study she completed was high school, at the convent where she was raised by nuns after her mother's early death. She then taught high school at the same convent high school for ten years. She later recalled that plants became an interest during her girlhood at the convent. It rang a bell for me, the lonely creative mind looks out the window and finds an ecosystem offering a world of color and life that had been varnished, cleaned, and tidied out of the interior spaces. In that world outside the convent, she heard the calling of these Western plants and they held her in their thrall until the day she died.

As I hiked along, the smell of wet soil and the sound of waterfalls accompanied my own search for more plant species. I was trying to see individuals more clearly on these walks. I spied and jotted down the big leaf maple and the California huckleberry.

An autodidact, Eastwood studied *Grey's Manual* and *The Flora of Colorado,* became an expert on the plants of Colorado. Perhaps one of the more illuminating stories I had come across was her selection, in 1887 at the age of twenty-eight, to guide Alfred Russel Wallace on a walk up Grays Peak at the height of the alpine flowering season. Eastwood had spent every summer when school was out, walking the mountain, collecting and recording plant species. The high school principal had recommended her as guide. I imagine her sense of triumph and fear at this challenge. Wallace, then sixty-four, and Charles Darwin, codiscovered the principle of natural selection. Botanizing in Colorado was an extension of his global work to understand how and why plants got to be where they were. He was an internationally recognized botanist, evolutionist, identifier of the Wallace Line, and spiritualist.

As I sifted through the stories of Eastwood's life, I found myself returning to the work of Loren Eiseley. Professor Eiseley and I never met—he died in 1977 when I was still a school-girl. But one day I found him on a library shelf at the University of Michigan and we have been together ever since. He has travelled with me to Australia, Antarctica, London, Thailand, in a kayak on the Andaman Sea, and on countless slogs through countless dull security lines. He offered these lines from Shelley in his *The Firmament of Time,* "The splendours of the firmament of time/May be eclipsed, but are extinguished not;/like stars to their appointed height they climb,/And death is a low mist which cannot blot/The brightness it may veil." This is the epilogue to a section entitled, "How the World Became Natural." It is a question occupying my mind. How does a place become natural and when we are restoring a place to a more natural state—as some argue the Presidio indeed may be—what to make of it? It always feels like he is asking me how to equally live in a world of dreams and theories alongside the world of fact, bloody births, broken bones, and surgeries, fears of homelessness and starvation, all wrapped in beauty and desire and hope. Eiseley was born on the family homestead in Lincoln, Nebraska, which was established when the region was still a territory. *The Immense Journey* was published in 1946 and I have a 1957 hardcover edition, a precious book I found in a shop in a remote town on the South Island of New Zealand. The cover is blue and decorated with images of an ape, a bird, and a sun, in a style that recalls either cave paintings or a particular modernist iconography. Someone wrote in cursive, in a light-blue pencil, across the cover; most is illegible but the word *Enjoy* stands out, next to two kisses, xx.

Eiseley offers two epigraphs, the first from Thoreau, "Man can not (sic) afford to be a naturalist, to look at Nature directly, but only with the side of his eye. He must look through and beyond her." The second from William Temple, who had been Archbishop of Canterbury and published a wildly popular book about Christianity and socialism: "Unless all existence is a medium of revelation, no particular revelation is possible…" The book thus made me happy from the start, with those words beckoning me in.

The cover flap quotes a review from *Saturday Review* magazine; Eiseley's meditations "glow with the wisdom and originality of a scientist who has pondered the riddle of experience and possesses the eloquence to put his thinking into words." What I like about Eiseley is how he meanders across subjects and ideas, how he shares insights into how scientists wove the stories of how the world works, what nature is up to, while adding his own thoughts and reflections. In one essay, "The Real Secret of Piltdown," he explores Wallace and his central questions about what it means to be human.

Eiseley begins his essay on Wallace, Darwin, and evolution: "How did man get his brain?" The question haunted Wallace and others. He writes: "It is a question which has bothered evolutionists ever since, and when Darwin received his copy of an article Wallace had written on this subject he was obviously shaken. It is recorded that he wrote in anguish across the paper. 'No!' and underlined the 'No!' three times heavily in a rising fervor of objection." He points out how natural selection aligned with the Victorian conceit that their civilization was the apex of human achievement and thus argued other races with different customs must therefore be biologically inferior; how there was conjecture that primitive cultures were closer to apes than to humans; and how, consciously or unconsciously, Darwinists narrowed the divide between man and ape, using native cultures as a bridge or missing link. Eiseley writes how Wallace protested this missing link notion, which apparently got under Darwin's skin, too.

I thought about Eastwood living in those same times, her intimate connection to these conversations through her work, how the Western U.S. was her tabula rasa, a set of wild and free territories unmapped and unknown. Women had more latitude in the American West, could get jobs hogged by white men back east, could get a stronger hold in the sciences, in academia; social norms must have been hard to enforce, and women and others benefited from that freedom—to some extent. Maybe that's part of why they called it the Wild West—there was crazy shit going on out here! Women, people of color, folks walking up from Mexico. Wallace and Eastwood became lifelong friends after their walk up Grays Peak, and she would visit him and his wife in England years later and be welcomed as family. I knew from reading about her work that she engaged in fierce battles with the Academy of Sciences to preserve botany's place in the new museum when it opened in Golden Gate Park. (That new building was badly damaged and had to be destroyed after the 1989 earthquake.)

Wallace was born to a poor family and developed a passion for botanizing. The common braid holding Eastwood and Wallace—and Eiseley—is one strand innate curiosity, one strand indomitable urge to see for oneself, and one strand writer. For each of them it all perfectly wove into a speculation hewn from the poetics of form of what else lived on Earth.

For Eiseley, the poetics of discovery took the form of a search for post-glacial man in the Western U.S. For Wallace, the form was plucking at an imagined seam dividing species in what were called the Spice Islands. In this writing, Eiseley picks apart Wallace's work with native cultures, showing the reader how living with hunter-gatherer cultures lead Wallace to abandoning the white, industrialist conceit they were inferior. Wallace reported his observations that native cultures had intellectual capabilities far in excess of what they needed to maintain their relatively simple hunter-gatherer way of life, asking: "How then, was an organ developed so far beyond the needs of its possessor? Natural selection could only have endowed the savage with a brain little superior to that of an ape, whereas he actually possesses one but little inferior to that of the average member of our learned societies."

Eiseley was also taken with Wallace's insistence that artistic, mathematical, and musical abilities could not be explained on the basis of natural selection and the struggle for existence.

No doubt Eastwood had studied Wallace's clashing views on evolution as well as one of his central hypotheses, published in 1859, derived from studying flora and fauna in the islands separating Asia and Australia. Called the Wallace Line, this imaginary boundary runs between Australia and Asian islands and the mainland, marking the point where species differ on either side of the line.

As I research Wallace and Eastwood making their discoveries, I often have to close my eyes and settle my brain. They were searching for, finding, and processing information with a level of intellectual computation that gives me pause. Connections parsed, in the line of a leaf, the bark of a tree, the dip of a bird's wing. All signs to be read. Think of the world presenting itself this way, species as text, a history and a story. And you are the keeper and transmitter of the tales.

So. The Wallace Line. West of the line, all the species are derived from or similar to those found on the Asian mainland. East of the line, many of the species are of Australian descent. Along the line the two groups mix and there are species hybrids. I came upon a brief passage in *My Life: Letters and Reminiscences,* that succinctly shows Wallace doing a read of nature's texts: "In this archipelago there are two distinct faunas rigidly circumscribed which differ as much as do those of Africa and South America and more than those of Europe and North America; yet there is nothing on the map or on the face of the islands to mark their limits. The boundary line passes between islands closer together than others belonging to the same group. I believe the western part to be a separated portion of continental Asia while the eastern part is a fragmentary prolongation of a former west Pacific continent. In mammalia and birds, the distinction is marked by genera, families, and even orders confined to one region; insects of a number of genera and little groups of peculiar species, the families of insects having generally a very wide or universal distribution."

Wallace and Eastwood took the train to Graymont, Colorado, and stayed in a log hotel, setting out the next day accompanied by the manager of a local mine. The three set up camp in a hut, dividing the room with a blanket to create separate sleeping areas by gender. The next day, they reached the summit and were met with an explosion of blossoms—cascading across the alpine landscape.

In 1891, after a trip to California, Eastwood interviewed for a job at the California Academy of Sciences in San Francisco. She was hired and spent the next forty years of her career working there.

My own botanizing tools on Mount Tam were smartphone and notebook and as I headed back towards the parking lot, it seemed impossible that she worked so effectively with all of the encumbrances—those long skirts and corsets. I have seen photos of her, five feet tall, glasses, smiling, wearing the traditional women's wear of the era. What I find in Eastwood is a kindred spirit in learning. She explored this ancient art of botany, saw how human culture and plant culture were indelibly connected, in society with one another, saw the paramount importance of species diversity.

The first ancient documents from Babylonian sources, Homer's works, and the Old Testament described plants for their medicinal and other utilities. Aristotle placed plants between the animate and the inanimate. Theophrastus' treatise *Historia Planetarum* is considered one of the most important books of natural history in antiquity. I have read that Theophrastus continually revised the manuscript and it remained unfinished at the time of his death. One belief is that the text was actually teaching notes and never intended to be a book. In it, he describes 550 species of plants. He is noted as the first person to lay out a systematic explanation and classification of plants.

Not long after Thanksgiving, while wandering in a second-hand bookstore in San Francisco's Mission District, I spotted a turquoise book embossed with gold type, Alice Eastwood's *Wonderland,* by Carol Green Wilson. The book cost thirty dollars and when I got home, I found many of the pages had never been cut apart; that is, this copy of *Wonderland* had never been read. On the opening page, the author signed it: To Jane Muir, with best wishes, Carol Green Wilson. San Francisco, December 11, 1974. Two-thousand copies had been printed by the California

Academy of Sciences in 1955. Eastwood reportedly participated enthusiastically in this biography, spending many hours with the author, telling stories from her life. What strikes in reading the book is how the stories all maintain a certain tenor: Life is tough but good. Through thrift and hard work great discoveries can be made. A modest woman with a strong work ethic prevails in life. I pondered this bifurcated view.

Eastwood's work seems much more spiritual at its core, too complex for simple moralistic themes. Like the work of all great artists of the land, she brings often-occluded details to the surface of consciousness—perhaps calling for a kind of faith that as a great grid of industrialization crawled then and now across the land, a thinking person could locate herself in the details of the wild world, could see the edges of a leaf of grass as talisman.

A Handbook of the Trees of California, written by Eastwood, was published as part of a series of Occasional Papers of the California Academy of Sciences, and is number IX, published in 1905. I acquire a copy I cannot afford through a rare book dealer on the East Coast. The leather-bound book is fragile, and its cracking spine quickly sheds the leather cover as I open and close it to look through. It is a book cover that wants to be in a box in an archive, held with white cotton gloves. But the pages are meant to be read. I sacrifice the object for the act, a statement that could be the theme for many lives wound interminably in the act of writing and reading.

In the preface, Eastwood writes: "The pressing need of a popular manual of the trees of California is the reason for this little book. The aim has been to prepare a work, which, while giving all the information necessary for the identification of the different trees of our valleys and mountains, will yet be put into a book that can be carried into the field." The publication committee consisted of Leverett Mills Loomis, chairman, Alpheus Bull, and Joseph W. Hobson. This is a limited edition of 500 copies and was signed by Alice Eastwood herself. The precise language of the book being,

This Edition is limited to five hundred copies numbered and
signed by the Author
[Signature]
This being
Number
162

Eastwood said the aim was to create a book, "so brief and
concise that the entire matter can be put into a book that can
be carried into the field." She offers good advice to all her
fellow observers and recorders of the outdoors: "Throughout
the work the aim has always been brevity and clearness—the
desire to help rather than to shine." It is a list. You can see
her at work, her mind ticking along. I had read that she once
wrote, in response to an academic who questioned her use of
multicolored planter boxes for an educational display of flowers
at the Academy, that he was some hidebound stickler for
system where system is not the desirable feature.

I called the California Academy of Sciences, now housed
in a building designed by Renzo Piano and set up an
appointment to view its Eastwood archives. I had read
versions of how she singlehandedly saved the seed collection
after the 1906 earthquake ruined the Academy, then on
Market Street. She had raced to the building, as fires marched
across the city unabated, where she found the main staircase
destroyed. Eastwood climbed the spindles and bannister as a
ladder, scaling it to the second floor in her long heavy skirts.
She found her seed collections, climbed back to the street
level and found someone with a cart to help her move them
out of harm's way. The collections would have represented
months if not years of her life in the wild, staring, poking,
and cataloguing. The building was entirely destroyed by the
fire. While the new Academy was built in Golden Gate Park,
she traveled, working in the Royal Botanical Gardens at Kew
and the British Museum. Joseph Dalton Hooker, the founder
of geographical botany, had also been an Antarctic explorer
and friend of Darwin's; Hooker traveled on the HMS *Erebus*

with James Ross to what is now called the Ross Sea, the most southerly voyage then to date.

I pulled on my coat and grabbed a thermos of tea and walked to Golden Gate Park from the Presidio, down Arguello, taking in the full design experience, two great urban forests joined via a boulevard. The Academy is a vibrant global research center, whose focus in the 21st century represents the slowly expanding language of climate chaos, sustainability, species diversity, conservation. A museum is tucked alongside and when I stepped inside, the soaring ceilings, a slice of rainforest ecosystem captured in a multi-story transparent ball, I sensed Eastwood, how this was the place her perseverance and work had started and allowed, that day of climbing the ruined staircase. And now all this.

The archives staff had assembled a selection of Eastwood's materials on a cart and they set me up at a table then left me alone to poke through it. I sat in the bright light. This is a particular moment, the moment of materiality. My extra hours of reading about her life paid off, which I had first found when doing my Antarctic research, to read about how things were made or used or cherished then to find them in some dark storage box, then to touch them and see the handwriting. I was excited but conflicted. What can be distilled from a few boxes of someone's things?

I saw knitted items she had made for a friend's child, a very precise bit of knitting, with an even gauge and a strong color sense. I held the aging wool, wrapped in tissue in an archivist's box. Her knitting was part of the archive of her scientific work. It felt more like an installation piece: baby clothes made by famous scientists. Did they show this to me because I taught at an art school? Maybe they felt because I was not a scientist, I could identify with the knitting. Maybe they simply loved it and wanted someone else to love it, too. I did not ask for an explanation.

Eastwood never married, although not because she was not asked. She had her field work and a prestigious post at the Academy. The seeds needed her full attention, they had their own stories to tell and she had to capture them. She had collected the seeds, sorted the seeds, classified the biota. The seeds became kin.

Many species were gone by the time Eastwood arrived in California. Naturalists who preceded her offered breathtaking reports of prairies filled with elk, grizzlies, and pronghorns in the valleys west of Mount Diablo, a mere thirty miles east of San Francisco. However, these same early naturalists, sent out with European expeditions to probe new places, held onto a more medieval view of the man/nature relationship, one that considered wild nature and humanity inimical, that is, harmful, hostile, or unfriendly. Duplicating systems and places familiar to them—Spain, France, the East Coast of North America— they quickly dug in with farms and orchards, with grazing herds and back filled bogs and built over buried creeks. John Muir, who later became Eastwood's friend and correspondent, arrived in 1868 and immediately asked to be pointed to the path east and out of San Francisco. He then walked east to Yosemite.

NOTEBOOK ELEVEN

Abiologist spotted *arctostaphylos franciscana*—a manzanita thought to be long gone from the Presidio—living in the wild when an old road was being torn down as part of the Presidio renovation. He spied it, actually and unbelievably, while driving through the Presidio on Highway 1, zooming towards the Golden Gate Bridge. Imagine it—car barreling along towards Marin, its driver looking intently out the windshield and then side windows, scanning the mayhem of road construction—the rusty rebar, the churning cement mixers, the huge yellow earth movers like industrial insects foraging, the freshly exposed hills, the dull greenish blues of serpentine rock.

I imagine he was thinking, massive tear downs of highways promise big reveals for biologists and botanists and there are only a few species that choose to grow on the toxic slab called serpentine. Picture him glancing back at the road, scanning the construction area, drifting a bit out of his lane, as he spotted it, could it be? Then hear someone laying on a horn, screaming, *watch where you are going, pal.*

The biologist wouldn't care about that, would he? Lost to the here-and-now of the road because he had just seen a ghost, in the form of a great carpet of *arctostaphylos franciscana.*

If I were filming this scene, for the beginning of a film about the Presidio and Alice Eastwood's life and, yes, we could say, how we place ourselves in the wild and what we do there, I would have him pull over, hit his hazard lights, look in the rear-view mirror, and then jump out and run to the guard rail. He would lean way over, then look up at the sky, a brilliant clear-blue Northern California sky with eyes alive with wild excitement—the look that comes with discovery.

Here is what transpired: *arctostaphylos franciscana* was quickly given legal protection. The Wild Equity Institute, the Center for Biological Diversity, and the California Native Plant

Society—filed an emergency petition for Endangered Species Act protection.

Meanwhile, botanists confirmed its identity and cranes arrived to move a 25,000-pound chunk of soil holding the manzanita to a habitat similar to its wild site.

One plant cannot regenerate a genetically diverse population of its species, nor does a colony of one species make a functional ecosystem.

The news: Daniel Gluesenkamp, cofounder of the Bay Area Early Detection Network, which coordinates response to newly introduced invasive weeds, made the discovery. "There's a few of us watching the roadsides," he says, "and when there's a big change, it's interesting."

Franciscan manzanita. Manzanita an American word, derived from the Spanish, manzana for apple. *Arctostaphylos franciscana.* A species with leathery bark, low stature, and a small ovoid leaf. About 1910, when Eastwood gave the species its official Linnean name, there were only three examples of *arctostaphylos franciscana* in the wild. All were in San Francisco. By 1947, *arctostaphylos franciscana* was overrun in the wild by human activity, its fate to be forever confined to lonely patches in private and botanical gardens.

And so that seemed to be the end for *arctostaphylos franciscana.* As humans spread out like a thick membrane across the terrain, flora judged lacking in ecstatic aesthetics or inspiration (that they conjured as then made into something else—food, fuel, medicine, tea, amusements)—were simply removed from the biosphere. Manzanita wood is notoriously bad to work with—splitting across the grain, generally refusing to be made into spoon or cupboard.

As I am working on this book, more than 190 nations met in Nagoya, Japan, to talk about ensuring the survival of diverse species. According to an article in *The New York Times* this survival looks grim because of pollution, exploitation, and habitat encroachment. Scientists increasingly plead that more needs to be done more quickly or else species extinctions will spike and our intricately connected natural world may vanish. More than 15,000 people came from all over the world to Nagoya for a meeting about species diversity. Some say we need to set aside vast tracks of land and ocean from development. Some say we are losing species at a rate 100 to 1,000 times the historical average, pushing us towards our sixth big extinction phase—the greatest since dinosaurs were wiped out 65 million years ago. If you just look at primates, of which we are one, almost fifty percent of the species are threatened—because of habitat destruction and hunting.

I wish Eastwood and Wallace were here, to wrap their big brains around these ideas. We have smartphones and smart cars but, I am told by a French sociologist, what we want is a sensitive phone and a sensitive car. Can you believe this, Eastwood? I can't believe it and I am here now, writing with a pencil on white paper, about a place that mattered to you. It is now a time when we want a phone to be sensitive.

In the 1940s when Eastwood said that "very few" of the species described in an 1816 expedition notebook still survived in the Presidio, she noted they had been killed by the "dense forest of cypress, pine, and eucalyptus planted years ago." (Later searches in the Presidio led to discovery of four dozen of the eighty-two species collected in 1816.)

Then there is Big Spill. My journals suddenly take on a more reporterly feel. Dates. Numbers. As though environmental disasters can be contained by understanding numeric scale.

November 7

A cargo ship hit the Bay Bridge and spilled gallons of oil into San Francisco Bay.

November 9

The oil spilled totaled 58,000 gallons. Now the Oiled Wildlife Care experts are on the scene in the Presidio, and Baker Beach is closed. The National Park Service says the beach is closed to keep people safe. The oil can make us sick too, albeit given that we don't have feathers, less so. I don't believe them. I believe they want to keep us from seeing the carnage, the dead birds washing ashore.

November 27

Today a ring of slime. No slugs visible. 55 degrees at 7:45 a.m. No sign of the oil spill as I walk down the dunes to the beach. They have cleared out the ice grass on the dune-hill behind my house, cut down some trees. They are restoring this to the native habitat, which will be a rolling carpet of silvery green, low-lying plants that flower in the spring. This means there's now nothing there. It is bare-naked sand. Blowin' in the wind. Again I wonder, when was the sand allowed to be bare-naked? Must feel good, soaking up that West Coast heat. As I think about how happy the sand must be, it crosses my mind: I am a non-native species and that status cannot, will not change.

That night I dream: The female red-tailed hawk that nests in the cypress trees behind my home snared by a small boy with a crewcut. The boy is from Georgia. He keeps the hawk's head in water and begins to ready his killing tools, a knife. First, he decides to blind the bird. I watch from small scrub, and approach the boy. I talk him into letting the bird go, even though the boy is set on showing his father how he, too, can trap an animal.

I untie the bird and wrap it in a towel. The hawk shivers and cries. At home, I call wildlife rehabilitation centers to find the best home for a hawk snared and then set free. The hawk sleeps for many hours, fading into days. I check to see it is alive. When it awakens, there will be food to gather, moles, mice, some other small ground animal. In the dream I wonder how hard these will be to catch.

The next morning, I head down to Baker Beach. The hawk with its cinnamon tails floats in easy gyres above, unknowing of my weird dream from the night before. I stop and watch it float in the cold Pacific wind and recall how my friend Baden, a penguin expert, talked about how the second there is no ground predation, birds choose not to fly. Like penguins. Or kiwis. Or the now extinct moa. We romanticize flying, but it is hard work.

The dark teal surf gently rolls towards the shore, which is empty save me and the usual gang of professional dog walkers. They are a caste unto themselves in this city: Men and women who hire out themselves in the service of dogs who need to walk; dogs that would otherwise be trapped in homes and apartments all day. There are more dogs in San Francisco than children.

The dog walkers talk in loud voices. *Charlie, I told you to stay with the other dogs, you are the new dog. Elias, please get your ball. Ginger, heel.* They carry plastic sticks, slightly bowed, used to catapult tennis balls down the beach, for those dogs inclined towards this exercise.

I turn and look the other way, towards the Golden Gate Bridge. A lone woman stands near the tall rocks stretching, yoga-like moves. I head in her direction. Across the Pacific, 12,000 miles of water between us, Baden walked a beach on the eastern shore of New Zealand. The beach resembles this one, both its beauty and the lethal roll of the waves. People drown at his beach, as they do here. People need to wear wet suits and be strong swimmers, there and here. I have known him for thirty years. The beach of Sumner, New Zealand, where he liked to walk resemble this one. There was a large rock in Sumner my children liked to climb and after we walked with Baden he would make us tea at his little house and we would hear stories of Antarctic explorers. We had a joke, after I moved here to the Presidio, that if I raised my right arm on my beach walk in hello, he could see me in Sumner. I don't know why we both found this so funny, yet we did. Now he is ninety. We have a joke, that I can raise my hand on my beach walk and he can see me. My arm lifts from my side, a wave masked as a stretch.

EPISODE TWELVE

It is in vain to dream of a wildness distant from ourselves. There is none such. It is a bog in our brains and bowels, the primitive vigor of Nature in us, that inspires that dream. I shall never find in the wilds of Labrador any greater wildness than in some recess of Concord, i.e. than I import into it. —Henry David Thoreau, *Journal,* August 1856

Geography is the study of the whole world while chorography is the study of its smaller parts. —Ptolemy

Reflecting eighteenth century antiquarian approaches to place, which included history, folklore, natural history and hearsay, the deep map attempts to record and represent the grain and patina of place through juxtapositions and interpenetrations of the historical and the contemporary, the political and the poetic, the discursive and the sensual; the conflation of oral testimony, anthology, memoir, biography, natural history and everything you might ever want to say about a place. —Mike Pearson and Michael Shanks, Theatre/Archaeology (Routledge 2001)

December: On Chorography

It is a hot, clear December morning in the Presidio and trust me these are not three words that you want to string together in this forest. We are in a deep drought, and we are all feeling it. Outside my sliding glass door, which looks west towards the Farallons which should be obscured by weather and are crystal clear, an Anna's hummingbird sees me inside sipping tea and does its unique cross-shaped presentation for my benefit. It is not saying, *Good morning, writer,* it is saying, *Get out here, sister, and turn on your fountain.* They all need the fountain, the birds, the squirrels and at night the raccoon family that knocks each other over to get there like some Keystone Cops routine.

I do what the hummingbird tells me to do and as the creaky
tap turns and the waterfall begins, I look out across the bank
of dunes and then down to Baker Beach. It's a world view that
everyone can agree is stunning. It is a view that forms the main
line of conversation in this place when friends gather and it is
clear and sunny or the sun is setting or it is raining and cold.
It is a view so pristine there is no weather that can alter human
perception. It is always beautiful.

The red-tailed hawks are banking and biding their time over
the dunes. The ice grass was carefully pulled as was the New
Zealand spinach, and the many of straggly cypress trees were
pulled down, opening up a field of play for indigenous plants
that had long been hanging by a fine thread. It feels right,
this new look, in part because when we do get rain it yields a
blooming spring. These unimpressive grey plants create a burst
and range of color, subtle and extreme. I take it all in and turn
to go back inside, but not before the hummingbird buzzes my
head. It does not feel like *thank you*. It feels like *you better not
turn off your hose, lady.*

In the kitchen, I wait for my children to come home from
their varied afterschool diversions—the older one can drive
now and is applying to colleges, and the two of them cruise
around town in my old purple car. *Who needs me,* I think. And
for some reason, this makes me feel quite content.

I turn my attention to the work at hand: Brassica is a genus
of plants that includes mustard, broccoli, cauliflower and,
sitting on my kitchen counter, the vivid green romanesco.
Before I slide it into a hot oven to roast, before I delicately
baste it with olive oil, cumin, coriander, paprika, and salt,
I take a moment and admire its singular beauty. Its tightly
packed florets are an example of a complex design that
exemplifies phllotaxis, a fractal pattern that can happen in
nature. It is a chaotic pattern of nature; these patterns are
found in seashells, distant galaxies, and when divided into
smaller pieces, you get infinite smaller versions of the whole.
The romanesco is a Fibonacci or golden spiral, a logarithmic

spiral where each quarter turn is farther from the origin by a factor of phi, the golden ratio. And I am going to eat it.

While the romanesco roasts, I turn to a project that is, shall we say, long overdue: The digitization of my Antarctic photos. There are many chromes and color negatives, and this is a rabbit hole for me: No sooner do I create a method for sorting the images than I am looking at each one, recalling when it was shot. I have my shot notebook nearby, and not far away is the Olympic OM1-n that enabled these images. So. I hold the film in their plastic sleeves and in their plastic slide cases to the light and once again, I am walking in Antarctica.

When traveling in Antarctica in summer, the sun moves in an easy counterclockwise circle around the sky and never sets. This fact alone—sunlight at 3 a.m.—keeps the sense of wild nature, the lush loss of self into a world too odd and different to grasp other than as a whispered cry, I am alive.

For those of us who come from the part of the world that associates cold with darkness and a setting sun at 4 p.m., well all this light and ice acts as a revelation. As a photographer, this new-look wild place demanded I cast aside preconceived notions about when the light would be "right." Forget rising and setting of sun. Sun hovering over Mount Erebus, Mount Discovery, White and Black Islands, tinkering with ideas of the known world, whispering in the poet's language, the real world goes like this.

I'd arise at 1:30 a.m. and go for a walk to Robert Falcon Scott's aging, grey-wood, fossil of a hut at Cape Evans and take pictures. Antarctica took on a feel of the familiar that to this day, I cannot shake. When I see it depicted on historic preservation sites or in museums I usually feel they have it, somehow, wrong. It defies such simple human logic and description. It is complex, like the concept of the phllotaxis.

The thing is, the way we people tinker with the story of places, framing and developing a rational line of argument, is worthy of some reflection. For what is it in the face of all the chaos: Plates slide around, mountains grow, ground liquifies, ice calves, we live in a dynamic environment. We live the dream of a stable Earth and stable climate, and yet we live the story of place, not the place as fact. What if we were to embrace the idea of change, relish instability and design our lives around this; to evolve into nomads whose strength is in mobility. Maybe we can find more dynamic patterns for human life in the patterns that wrap themselves around us. I sit back in my bright blue and steel office chair, acquired for five dollars at the University of Iowa Surplus furniture and gear warehouse one grey autumn day. Not long after the Antarctic Treaty's creation in 1961, a successful international effort to spare the continent for peaceful scientific exploration and discovery, Benoit Mandelbrot introduced the concept of the fractal, which has similar shape properties at all levels of magnification. Clouds, coastlines, canyons, ferns, and strange attractors are all united in their fractal design. That there is a marvelous coherence and agreement across clouds and snowflakes about their structure and design.

It started as a rainy and grey winter in the Presidio and then the clear sky came blasting out of the west. Now it is a perfect day for walking to *Spire*, a sculpture designed and built by Andy Goldsworthy that was completed in 2008. Years later, it is slowly turning more silver bringing to mind the Antarctic hut built by the Scott party. Trees will be trees and wood will be wood when exposed to sun and water and wind.

I am meeting my friend and teaching partner Mara because she is someone who can and will drop everything to walk around in the woods and talk about art and trees. She's from Idaho and has this hardscrabble approach I appreciate. As we start out on our walk, she digs her hand into a rotting tree stump and pulls out some wet, sludgy wood: Here, she says, you can use this to draw. It's great material for making art.

Mara's husband, Steven, who was a prominent industrial designer and the editor of *i-D* magazine for many years; I never knew him when he was not very sick. The nature of his illness is not my story to tell, but let us say it was epic and had only one possible outcome. He knew it, she knew it, and yet they remained busy making things like books and exhibitions with this lurking clock.

We all have a clock, Mara once said and then gestured to Steven snoozing on the couch. It's just that we can see ours. She said things like this with a strange and beautiful courage and if I pointed this out she would scoff at me and say, *I am from Idaho and we don't think that way.* We don't get to meet too many brave people, day to day, and the funny thing is that they look like all the rest of us. I know Céline said this more poetically and I don't care. Steven I remember not for the scope of his prodigious maladies but for his love of place, language, and form. And, of course, words.

We set out walking up a short, steep, muddy path to *Spire.* A single red-tailed hawk, *buteo jamaicensis,* hovering. Red-tailed hawks are not on any endangered-species lists. They adapt and live where they want. Their cinnamon tails are a daily sight for us in the Presidio and they have a sharp, knowing presence, sitting on light poles, watching for moles, rats, and mice. This hawk perches in a euc tree nearby, looking patiently for something to grab and eat. Flying burns a lot of calories.

By the time I knew him, Steven was toughing it out on a daybed in their sunny living room overlooking the Cathedral of Saint Mary of the Assumption, a church designed in the late 1960s by a group of architects including Pietro Belluschi, then dean of the MIT School of Architecture, constructed during the ebullient days of Vatican II. Its local nickname is the Washing Machine Agitator and from a distance the agitator would seem to be the aesthetic inspiration in its twisting, enormous central form rising towards the sky.

When I would pop by to head out with Mara for a walk or sushi at Kabuto, Steven is there, creating black notebooks of clippings and images and notes. He always inquires about Antarctica and the Presidio and he always had come across information about one or both places and he would share it all with me. Because, as we liked to laugh, *why find bits and scraps of things if they are not for some friend trying to get their fucking books done?*

Mara walks in the trees that surround *Spire*, trees planted more ten years ago, some by my children when they were school age. The trees are huge now and one day they will mask the spire from view, as designed by Goldsworthy. The forest will absorb the work, embracing the trees that once grew somewhere in this reserve, thirty-seven Monterey cypress affixed in a twelve-foot pit, sealed in with concrete. According to the text describing the work, *Spire* is "inspired by church bell towers."

Mara used to teach a class with Steven that brought students into the Presidio, biology as master metaphor, and they gathered students here to be inspired and to have what Mara states in a loud voice *BIG IDEAS*. Mara wanted them to study the design of tree branching systems, masterful schemes in and of themselves. As she talks, I point out the sick, old trees that line the golf course—they are less than twenty percent canopy and look like some cartoonish trees from a children's book; they are the result of crowding and pressing towards open sky for the nourishment of photosynthesis. I remind Mara that I spent a lot of time with Peter Ehrlich, who had been a lead forester for many years in the Presidio, and when he was helping Andy build *Spire* he would invite me around to watch. Peter was a good colleague in trees and poetics.

We are standing in a 100 percent artificial place, Mara adds, pointing to the adjacent golf course, half hidden by the forest. Yet the materials used are natural, and the forces of nature are at work on all of it. She has photos, she notes, of where golf balls have left interesting marks on the trees, a whole series of photos showing how a more obviously human-made environment scars the less-obviously human-made forest.

We walk away from *Spire*, down along West Pacific, the road where scions of San Francisco society have long held homes along the Presidio wall. The trees along West Pacific were carefully groomed over the years so as to not obscure the magnificent views of the Golden Gate from the masses. Thus the trees along this walk have a different feel entirely, the feeling I get from bonsai or hedge mazes. Land slaves groomed to perfection. This line of trees leads to another Goldsworthy piece that is more ephemeral, *River of Wood.* I recall when Peter told me how they saved cut eucs so that Goldsworthy could fit them all together into this flow. The trunks spill down the hill astride a path called Lover's Lane, the story being this is the path the soldiers followed out of the fort and into town to meet sweethearts.

It has been a long time walking in the Presidio and as I gaze across the houses on this eastern edge of the park, past the dwarf cypress trees made so by rich people who insisted they be trimmed to allow a view of the Golden Gate Bridge and the Army complied, past the new baseball diamonds and the dug-out creek and the place where they say the ruins of Juana Briones's home is, towards the north and west, the forest feels both boundless and incredibly small, a stand more than a forest, a last stand at the edge of world.

While it is a forest and not an estate of my own design, it is also a place that feels very much a part of me in a peculiar manner. I have never tried to be an expert on all the details of the Presidio nor have I wanted to imagine a world where the only way I would leave here is feet first, as they say. I think about ideas of place from many hundreds of years ago when we knew a place through folklore and natural history and shared truths and I think how the Presidio after all of these years of walking and looking has seeped into my seams in a particular way and how all of these walks are indeed interpenetrations and how in the forest there is no seam between, to quote Pearson and Shanks, "the discursive and the sensual." I guess all of these pieces of scrap both need to be heaved skyward to vaporize into the atmosphere and to be sewn like sequins onto a particular ornate jacket. In the end this is everything I might want to say about the place called Presidio.

Mara wants to know how I hold so many stories and facts about these trees—(while she had been walking I have been spouting off tree and *Spire* facts like some bookie calling out the odds for an upcoming race.) How the trees of *Spire* were gathered from those culled as part of the forest thinning. How this gave them a chance to stand and reach for the sky in some version of perpetuity. How they are held together with a tool

called a come-along and how it is the only Goldsworthy piece that he did not actually build himself. How the federal lawyers made them dig a deeper pit so

Spire is designed to slowly vanish into the trees that surround it.

that *Spire* would not fall over in the wind storms of winter and squash a walker. I tell her about walking to the site in the early morning during construction and how I would watch Andy watching them make this sculpture but how I was too shy to say hello to him. I point to the red-tailed hawks and talk about their resilience and wonder why and how they adapt so readily when other species cannot or will not. I ask if she thinks environmental adaptation is a choice, like writing or not writing is a choice, and she says she needs to think about that and then we are silent for a spell, standing by *Spire* and taking it all in. The site exudes a feeling of evanescence, but I think this and do not speak it because some things in nature are best not named aloud. Instead, because it is getting late and the sun will soon leave us, I say, *time to walk*.

NOTEBOOK 12

Not every book about nature and walking comes with a playlist. But this one does. I write this in blue pen on a creamy opening page of yet another journal, sitting at the Steelcase desk. There are shelves of journals now and most are half empty. I like buying them more than writing in them, I guess. I scribble my playlist. However the first rule is never listen to music while walking in the woods. Bad idea. First of all, it creates an unnecessary interiority. The woods are there for you, ready to take you away. But. Once home: To get going, Earth Wind and Fire, Dancing in September and Boogie Wonderland; to stop and reflect, George Harrison, My Sweet Lord; to get going again, Rob Base and DJ EZ, It Takes Two; to reflect, Eric Clapton, "Layla"; David Bowie, Young American; to internally argue whether there is one *greatest rock song of all time* and it is by Cheap Trick, I want you to want me; to remember Maryland, Little Feat and Marshall Tucker and yes, the Bee Gees and Stevie Wonder; to remember Detroit, Eminem, *8 Mile,* and Fleetwood Mac; to feel beauty and pain and loss, Elvis Costello, and Etta James; to think about beauty and persistence and general badassery, Ella Fitzgerald and Peggy Lee and the Nick Cave; to inject a moment of *yes, I am alive* to writing, Crowded House, Don't Dream It's Over, and Biggie Smalls, Going Back to Cali and/or Abba, Dancing Queen; to wonder why some people get to have such great voices, Tracy Chapman and Pavarotti singing duets; monks doing covers of U2, I Still Haven't Found What I'm Looking For; to continue wondering, in this case why the best people die young, Charlie Parker; to think about how folk music is divine across all borders, Zoltán Kodaly; and of course and always, when I have to absolutely, completely simply get some lines laid down and move forward, Led Zeppelin. Livin', lovin': She's just a woman. Or at least that is how I think it is punctuated. As I make this list, I know to stop while I am ahead. And so I head outside into a misty, silver afternoon.

I clamber up the narrow, euc-leaf coated slippery trail, hop the guard rail, and start walking north on Washington Boulevard. I have lived here for more than 12 years and in that time the rent has nearly doubled. I don't know how much longer I can, as a writer, realistically call the forest home—and at this point there is nothing else to call myself. I am stuck with writing and vice versa. And this makes me feel a combination of elation, poignancy, sadness, contentment, happiness, despair, and resolute calm, that is, a typical day. I thought this book would keep me from traveling farther afield and in the end it did not; I have been out and about to Australia, New Zealand, Iceland, and Antarctica. So much for working close to home. My children have moved out, and I live here alone. *I miss them every day.* I stop and pick up a euc blossom cap and breath in its rich minty scent. There is nothing like the real thing. As I think those words, I know they are pop music and advertising lingo, and yet they are words that work. *The real thing.* The real thing is that it took more than ten years to conceive of and write this book so much for getting this done pronto and getting back to Antarctica. I stop and admire how the lichens have spread over the last couple years, across rocks and branches.

Lichens are appealing. They offer a quiet presence, almost an ornamentation, to the more distinguished trees. They encrust rocks and stump and limb not far from my front door, and I know that part of the lush experience of a walk in the woods comes from being in their presence. I reckon this is in part because of what they are, as scientific fact. Lichens are algae and fungus that team up and survive together. Symbiotic relationship. I have always loved that word, symbiotic, which comes from the Greek, for living or dwelling together. I would hazard a guess that there is much to learn from the lichen as we humans head into climate chaos. The algae is subservient, so they say, to the fungus, producing carbohydrates for the fungus to consume. The algae cells are woven into the fungus. Yet who can say who has the upper hand in this relationship?

Peter was a forester who worked in the Presidio and who became my friend. He used to text me and point out places where I could see Presidio raptors in action, where they were storing felled logs, general thoughts on the poetics of place. Not everyone frames the world around places they love and I have come to cherish and relish those who share my passion. He was also the poet of the forest and sometimes sent bits of Yeats, "Young man, lift up your russet brow,/And lift your tender eyelids, maid/And brood on hopes and fears no more." He told me how the keystone tree for *Spire* was an 110-year-old Monterey cypress: All the others were moved into place and secured using a man-made device called a come-along. We walk at 6:30 a.m. and he describes the steel sleeve that holds *Spire,* it is four feet in diameter. The rock surrounding it is serpentine, which has chrysotile in it, which is where the asbestos is, and when the asbestos gets wet it is a sticky, awful clay.

In 1841 Ralph Waldo Emerson published *Circles:* "Our life is an apprenticeship to the truth, that around every circle another can be drawn; that there is no end in nature, but every end is a beginning; that there is always another dawn risen on midnoon and under every deep a lower deep opens." Major Jones, the park designer and poet of place, would have been aware of Emerson and transcendentalism, of what Whitman and others had to say in those times about nature. He would have been aware that the Northeast's forests had been largely felled and people were gnashing teeth about how railroads altered life in unexpected and unwanted ways, including the standardization of time. Time keeping had been a religious experience, held by the town parson, setting the town clock. Then the railroad companies muscled in, cutting through the slight hollows and valleys overgrown with cone flowers, birds being dispersed and trees shoved aside.

We both loved owls. Pete had kept tabs on a great-horned owl, who had built a nest a short walk from my front door. When the owlets were big enough to get pushed out of the nest to practice life, I would wander down over to watch with loving attention for a period of a few minutes to several hours.

This is how it went one day in the woods: The mother owl nudges the owlets out of the nest and they flutter-plop down to the soft forest floor, piled with curvilinear euc leaves. They pop around—two puff balls with eyes. They are impossibly cute. The crows come, what Peter called the gangstas of the woods. The crows like to harass the raptors. The puffball owls are an easy target. I feel tremendously agitated. The crows are hopping around, circling the owlets, cawing. I wonder what the mother is thinking: Enough of the tough-love, scared-straight approach, I say out loud. Then, as though we are in dialogue, the mother comes whizzing down from the nest. She descends swiftly and with intent, talons fixed. She rips the head off of one of the crows. The end. All of the other crows disperse. The babies take it all in. The mother returns to the nest. I walk to the edge of the dunes and look out past the cliffs called the Golden Gate to the Farallon Islands. They are knife edges against a lemon sky. Then I turn and head towards home. *Here is where I walk.*

ACKNOWLEDGMENTS

The Presidio is a marvelous forest, and everyone should come and walk and more generally advocate for and celebrate our shared open spaces and trees. These places belong to each and all of us, shared. Allowing ourselves to give each other open space and ecosystems means there is abundance to receive for all of us. I am grateful to the volunteers and underpaid civil servants who tend and design and advocate for the Presidio and indeed all of the world's public parks and open spaces. I want to thank *The Bellevue Literary Review* for publishing my essay, "How Air Moves," and Laura Julier and *Fourth Genre* and W. Scott Olsen and *Ascent* for publishing pieces of this when I needed a spur. Christopher Merrill and Donald Morrill: Thank you. Caroline Hurwitz, Jennifer Harper, Jennifer Morla, Mara Holt Skov, and Linda Fornaciari: for walking miles and taking the weight off at just the right time. And to my extended family, in particular Peter and Yumi: for their unconditional love and support.

My day job as a college professor and administrator is made better because of my creative colleagues at California College of the Arts. I thank my many students in Design and Writing for their curiosity and vibrance, which has been a terrific spur.

Among the people who passed when I was writing this book were the forester and poet Peter Ehrlich, who was so kind and generous to me and read many of these pages; and the historian Baden Norris who taught me to write histories that privileged ordinary people and simple gestures in nature.

I am deeply grateful to Alrica Goldstein, Sara Hendricksen, Justin Race, and the University of Nevada Press team. Thank you for saying yes. Your work making books is a gift and a blessing and the trees, slugs, coyotes, and ghosts herein offer gratitude for sharing these stories.

ABOUT THE AUTHOR

Leslie Carol Roberts was born in New Jersey and grew up in Maryland and Michigan as her family moved often for her father's work as a journalist. She earned a BA from University of Michigan, an MFA from the University of Iowa Nonfiction Writing Program, and an MA from the University of Canterbury.

Roberts' book about reporting on Greenpeace in Antarctica and then researching south polar presence across museum and book culture, *The Entire Earth and Sky: Views on Antarctica,* was published by University of Nebraska in 2008 and by Bison Books in paperback in 2012. Her work has been anthologized, including *On Nature* (Penguin Tarcher.) As a journalist and essayist, Roberts has been widely published in newspapers and magazines in the US and abroad, including *The Sydney Morning Herald,* the *Nation* (Bangkok), the *Baltimore Sun,* the *Christian Science Monitor, Forbes FYI, Ascent,* the *Bellevue Literary Review, Fourth Genre,* the *Iowa Review* online, and *Punctuate.*

Roberts is a featured conference speaker on her scholarship of place and has been funded by a Fulbright Fellowship to New Zealand and a Fulbright Travel grant, among many other awards. Roberts has taught at the University of Iowa, Saint Mary's College of Moraga, and the California College of the Arts, where she is part of the Architectural Ecologies Lab, editorial director of the online literary magazine, *1111,* and professor and chair of the MFA Writing Program.